WE

PETER SCHUMANN

ISBN-13: 978-1-942515-77-7
Library of Congress Control Number: 2016961835
Fomite
58 Peru Street
Burlington, VT 05401

WE

ATTENTION!.

ATTEN-
TION.

ATTENTION !
POPULATION BEWARE !

WHEN MR PUNCH WAS
ELECTED TO BE THE BOSS
OF THE POPULATION & THE
POPULATION INSPIRED ITSELF
TO MAKE MR PUNCH THEIR
BOSS THEY GAVE HIM THE
PRESIDENTIAL PURPLE COAT
& THE TRADITIONAL CUDGEL
WITH WHICH TO PUNISH THE
UNWILLING & ALSO THE UN-
FITTING & TO ENABLE HIM
TO CUDGEL HIS WAY TO THE
VERY VERY TOP WHERE HE
NEEDED TO BE ACCORDING

TO HIS OWN JUDGEMENT.
& THEREFORE POPULATION BEWARE!
THOU MUST NOW ACT MINIMA—
LISTICALLY & ACCORDING TO THE
LAW OF THE LAND WHICH IS
MR. PUNCH'S CUDGEL!
& HENCEFORWARD THE POPULATION
WAS SEEN TO HAVE RED EARS
FROM SHAME & A PALE
COMPLEXION FROM THE
REQUIRED TASTE FOR PALENESS.
& MR. PUNCH MADE HIMSELF
AN ARMY OF POWERFUL COPS
ALL PROPERLY BUILT FROM CORN—
STARCH & PAPER LIKE REAL
PAPERMACHE. & WITH HIS
ARMY HE SET OUT TO FIX

ALL ROTTEN BANANAS & ALL
ROTTEN CIRCUMSTANCES & EVEN
THE ROTTEN POLITICS OF THE
LAND & OF MANY OTHER
LANDS

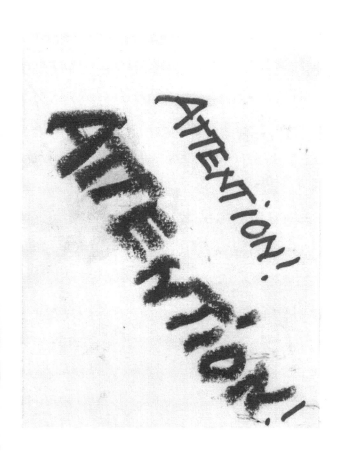

& NOW BEFORE
THE HEAVENS
HAVE A CHANCE
TO SERVE THEIR
FIRE & BRIMSTONE
IN RESPONSE TO
THE EARTHLINGS
STUPIDITY

& PROVIDE THE
DECEIVED POP-
ULATIONS WITH
REASONABLE &
MEASUREABLE
PUNISHMENTS
BY UNLEASHING
THE PROFESSIONAL
DEMONS OF
STORM &
CATASTROPHE

BY TOSSING THE
EARTHLINGS BACK
TO WHERE THEY
CAME FROM:-
GREATGRANDFATHER
DIRT & GREATGREAT
GRANDMOTHER
EARTH & EVEN EXCELLENT
ECONOMIC GROWTH

FACTORS & EMPLOYMENT STATISTICS
WON'T RETARD THESE LOGICAL
DEMONS WHO ARE NOT ORDERED
IN BY OPINION OR THOUGHT
BUT ARE ORDERED IN BY FACT

HOW MANY

23

24

28

30

THE POPULATION EFFECT IN YOUR DAY TODAY LIFE

REALIZING YOUR OWN POPULATION ANXIETY

THE ENORMOUS
DIFFICULTY TO
ACCEPT YOUROWN
POPULATIONSELF

DEATHS

deadliest yet

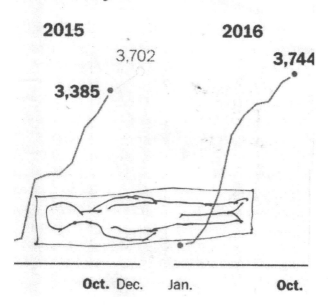

2015

3,702

3,385

2016

3,744

Oct. Dec.　Jan.　　　　Oct.

This year is on pace to be the

2014

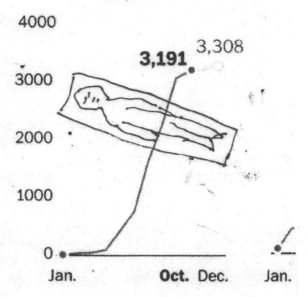

4000

3000 **3,191** 3,308

2000

1000

0

Jan.　　　　**Oct.** Dec.　Jan.

Migrants dead or

YEAR OF INCIDENT

2014   ○ 2015   ○ 2016

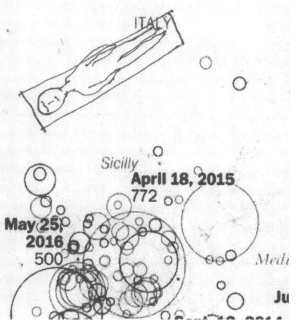

ITALY

Sicily

April 18, 2015
772

May 25, 2016
500

Medi

Ju

missing

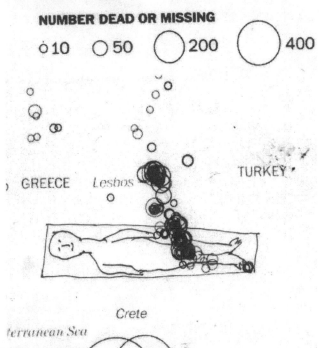

NUMBER DEAD OR MISSING

○10 ○50 ○200 ○400

GREECE *Lesbos* TURKEY

Crete

terranean Sea

ne 2, 2016
331

PART
ONE
PRIMARY
PAINTING

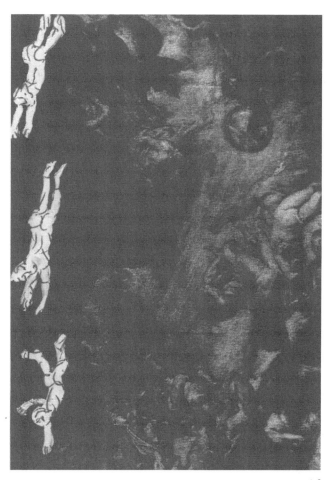

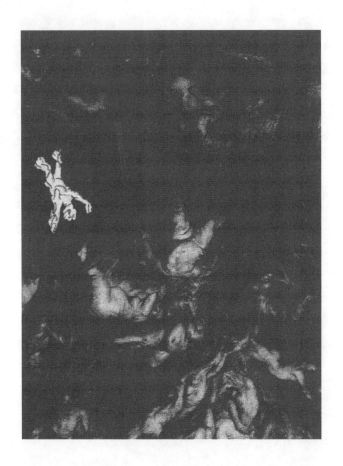

WINDOWS WHICH TOSS THEIR
SURPLUS FROM ABOVE
WAGONS WHICH UNLOAD
THEIR EXCESS LIFE DOORS
OF THE DARK SKY BURST
OPEN DISCARD WHAT THE
SKY DOESNT NEED

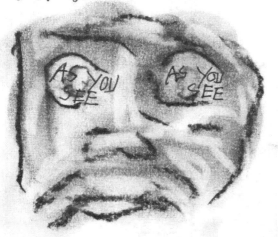

SUCH ARE THE FALLERS
FROM THE VOID THEY SPLASH
INTO THE MUDCRUSTED
UNDERNEATH THEY PLANT
THEIR HEADS INTO THE
ORIGINAL DEBRIS

PART 2

BIRTH

OF

FORMULA

TORN

THEY ARE THE SMASHED
NOTHING FROM ABOVE BEFORE
THEY ARE ASSIGNED LIFE
& BE THERE TO BE POPULATION
THEY WERE NOT EXPECTED
THEY ARRIVED UNEXPECTED
NO DESIGNER NO WISHFUL
THINKING PRODUCED THEM
THEY FELL & FROM FALLING
THEY BECAME ROOTED &
UPRIGHTED TO BE POPULATION

OUR CONTINUOUS ALWAYS FALLING
AND NEVER ENDING BEING TOSSED
FROM ABOVE WHERE ALL THINGS
DON'T EXIST YET & GIVE US
THEIR HOPE INSTEAD

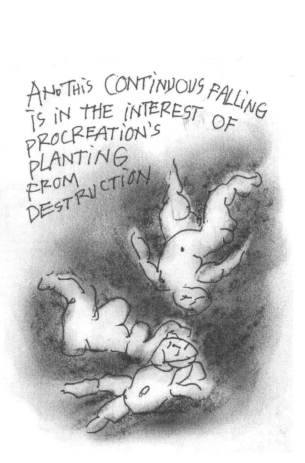

AND THIS CONTINUOUS FALLING
IS IN THE INTEREST OF
PROCREATION'S
PLANTING
FROM
DESTRUCTION

& IS A MAJOR INGREDIENT OF THE UNCONTROLLED OF OUR BRAIN OUR LIVES DOWNPOUR INTO WHICH ARE FASTENED

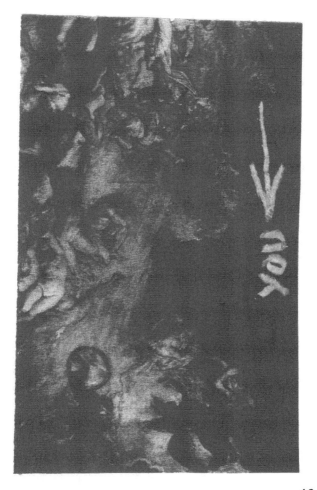

64

THE ALL IS IN THE ANIMALS

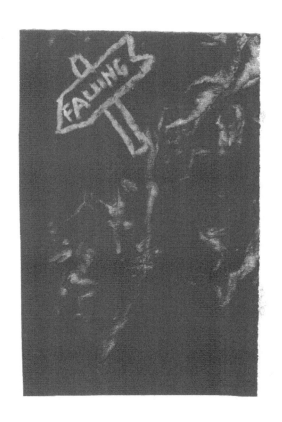

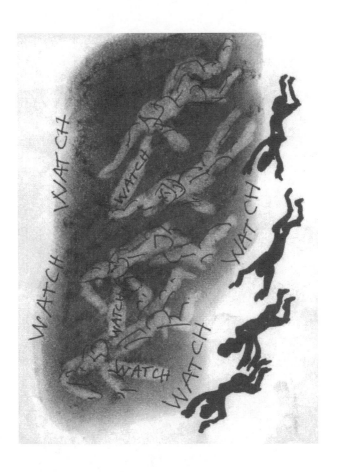

68

THE ALL IS IN
THE ANIMALS THE
CRAWLING FLYING
BOUNCING
PARADING
MAKING ALL
DANCES EQUAL
& SUFFICIENT
FOR ECSTASY'S
SAKE &
UNSTOPPABLY
PROGRESSING
TO ACHIEVE
FULL CIRCULAR
BREADTH
&
COMPLETION

THE CRAWLING FLYING BOUNCING AND PARADING MAKING ALL DANCES EQUAL

AND SUFFICIENT FOR ECSTASY'S SAKE

AND AS THE ANIMALS
FALL THEY TURN HUMAN
& DESCEND INTO THE HUMAN
& ABYSS & PARTAKE IN THE
EMPIRE OF WILL &
STATUE THAT HAS
BEEN ACHIEVED

& AS THE HUMANS
JOIN THE ANIMALS
IN THE CHUTE THEY
COMPREHEND THEIR
SIBLINGS THE SNAKES
& MAMMOTHS FOR
THE FIRST TIME

JOIN THE BIRDS IN THE
CHUTE & COMPREHEND YOUR
SIBLINGS FOR THE FIRST TIME

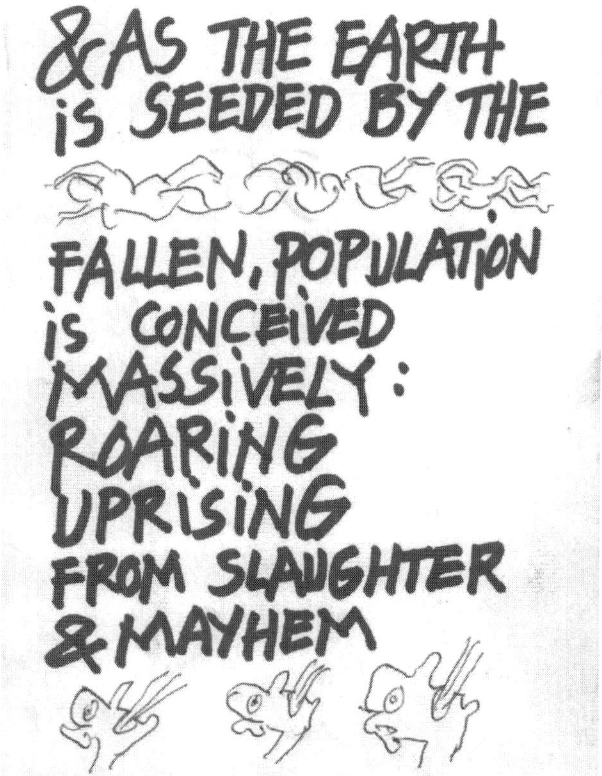

& AS THE EARTH
is SEEDED BY THE

FALLEN, POPULATION
is CONCEIVED
MASSIVELY:
ROARING
UPRISING
FROM SLAUGHTER
& MAYHEM

& WOUNDS AS LARGE AS
CRATERS SUPPLY BIRTHING
SPACE THE SPACE TO AFFORD
THE UPRIGHT THE ENTIRE
MEN & WOMEN WHO GUIDE
THE TODDLING MASSES
INTO DEFINITIVE MOTION
WORKFORCE MOTION &
AMBITION, INEVITABLE
SENSE & CONFINEMENT
THE ULTIMATE FATE

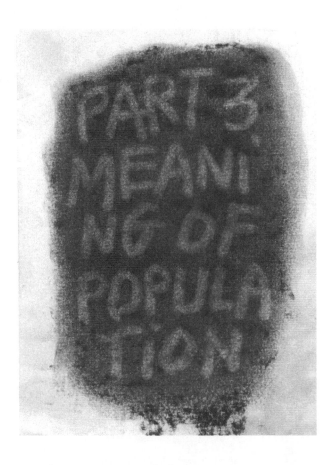

PART 3
MEANING OF POPULATION

AS THE EARTH IS SEEDED
BY THE FALLEN THE LIFE
THAT SPROUTS IN THE
UNDERNEATH PUSHES
UPWARD' IN ITS VERTICAL
STRIFE & FURNISHES
MEANING & FROM MEANING
POPULATION

& POPULATION RISES LIKE
THE RABBITS IN THE LUSH
GREENERY OF THE EARTH
& THEN IS THERE
UNQUESTIONABLY WOMAN
MAN CHILD OVER & OVER
AGAIN TILL THE MASSES
THAT SUPPLY WEIGHT
WITH MEANING CALL IT
BY ITS PROPER NAME:
POPULATION

& FROM THERE MORE
CORRECTLY = WORKFORCE
THE FORCE THAT IS
NEVER MIND THE RESULT
BUT IS AS FORCED AS
FORCE & WORK & THEREFORE
DESIGNATED WORKFORCE

& MUCH MORE THAN WOMAN
MAN CHILD IS REAL &
THEREFORE THE REALITY
OF NO LONGER MAN MAN
WOMAN WOMAN CHILD CHILD
BUT REAL AS IN FORCE
WHICH WORKS & IS THEREFORE
WORKFORCE ORDERED TO
SELF SACRIFICE FOR THE
ABSTRACTION WORK

NO MORE THAN THAT
NEVER MIND THE MAMMOTH
OR THE BIRD OR THE RESULT
IN SERVICE & SERVITUDE
TO SANCTIFIED HABIT

PART 4

DISSO
LUTION
OF POP
ULATION

THE MAIMINGS ILLEGITIMATE
& BOMBS LEGITIMATE & URGENTLY
RUNNING FEARS & THE
AGGRESSION OF LIGHT THAT
EXACTLY WHICH WAS THE
GOOD & THE DISPERSAL OF
LIFE'S HABIT INTO FURTHER
RUNNING AS IN SUFFERING
& HOLDING ON & LOSING &
DRAGGING & GRABBING &
GETTING AWAY BARELY &
DUCKING UNDER & TRYING
TO NOT BE THERE & SUCCEED
& STOP BEING

& STOP & NOT EXIST &
NONEXISTENT SEE & AS
SEER SEARCH FOR THE LOST
& IN THE LOST SEE MEANING

& POSSESS NOT & AS
NONPOSSESSOR PROCEED
INTO THE FIRM WHICH
IS THE STRUCTURE WHICH
IS THE EXCLUSIVE NORMALITY
WHICH DOES NOT SCREAM

& BY THE SAME TOKEN
YOU SCREAM NOT BUT
RECEIVE INSTRUCTIONS
& THEN BEHAVE TILL
PERMISSION IS GRANTED
TO APPLY & YOU APPLY FOR
LIFE FREQUENTLY &
FREQUENTLY REJECTED &
APPLY FOR LESS THAN LIFE
& FREQUENTLY REJECTED
YOU APPLY FOR EVEN LESS

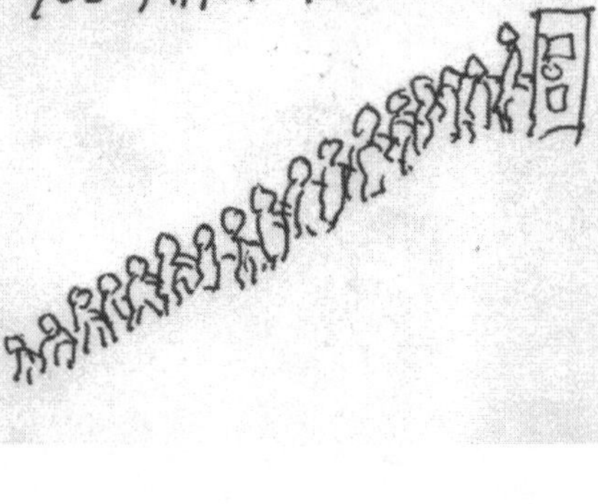

& FINALLY YOU APPLY
FOR REFUGEEDOM WITH
ITS UNRIGHTFULNESSES
& NONGUARANTEES

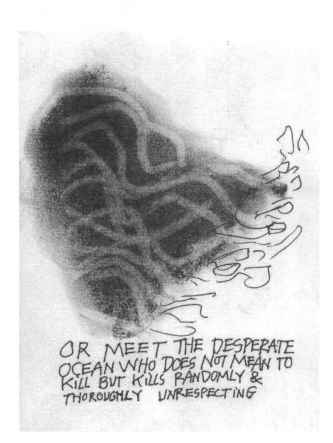

OR MEET THE DESPERATE
OCEAN WHO DOES NOT MEAN TO
KILL BUT KILLS RANDOMLY &
THOROUGHLY UNRESPECTING

UNNEEDED CHILD UNNEEDED
MOTHER CONFINED TO THE WAVE
THAT LIFTS THEM & DOWNS THEM
& CAN NEVER STOP LIFTING
& DOWNING THEM

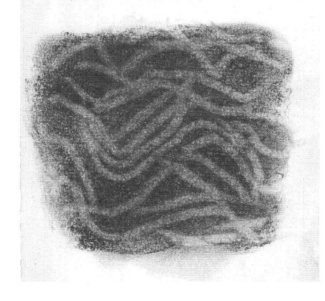

PART 5

POPULATIONS

INCARCERATION

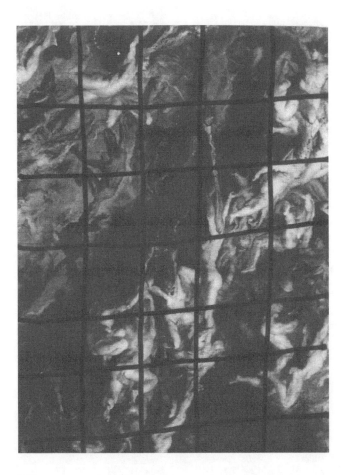

HUNGER THIRST DESIRE
ENVY COLD LOGIC PITY
ALL ACT DILIGENTLY TO
MAKE CRIME ATTRACTIVE
OR NECESSARY ONLY CRIME
CAN SATISFY HUNGER ONLY
CRIME CAN WARD OFF HURT
& FATALITY THE ORDER THAT
SCHOOLS & RULES THE DISCARDED
POPULATION ABANDONS IT
WHENEVER IT COLLAPSES FROM
ANY OF THE COMMON WEIGHTS
IT IS ASSIGNED TO BEAR

THE DISTILLATION OF ORDER
IS THE PRISONCELL
DESIGNED TO ISOLATE
THE UNCOMMON FROM
THE COMMON.

THE UNCOMMONER'S
SPACE AS DICTATED BY
THE UNCOMMON DETAIL
OF LIFE IS THE 6' X 9'
PRISON CELL CARVED
FROM THE DISORDERLY ALL

PART 6

POPULA
TIONS

RETHINK
ING

THE VITAL STUFF OF THE
POPULATION'S MIND & HEART IS
ITS FALLEN SUBSTANCE ITS
FROM FALLING DERIVED
SUBSTANCE WHICH EMBRACED
THE BIRDS IN ITS FALL FROM
THE VOID & NEVER STOPPED
KICKING & BREATHED
DEEPLY EVEN IN THE BOMBING
RAID

& DROWNED IN THE OCEAN
& RESUSCITATED & WAS NOT
CHAINED SUFFICIENTLY BY THE
ORDER OF THE FORCE WHICH
MEANT IT FOR ITS WORK

DROWNED
&
RESUSCITATED

& DID NOT ONLY WORK
BUT MANAGED TO SNEAK
OUT TO BREATHE ITS BREATH
OUTSIDE THE WORKFORCE
& DID NOT TOTALLY SURRENDER
TO POSSESSORSHIP & DID
NOT PROSTRATE ITSELF INFRONT
OF THE ABSTRACTIONS THAT
INDOCTRINATE ITS MIND
& SITS DOWN IN ITS GODDAM
SOLITUDE TO RETHINK ITS WHY

PART 7
POPULATION
NECESSITY

THE THEN POPULATION
DROWNING & SUCCUMBING
& CLIMBING FROM THE WRECKAGES
OF CONDEMNATION

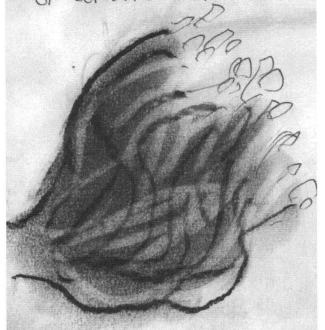

DID NOT SUFFICIENTLY
RESURRECT THE OBVIOUS
WHICH IS THE ALL WHICH
IS DOOMED LIKE THE
REFUGEEDOM OF THE
DISCARDED POPULATION
& CANNOT GAIN RIGHT
OR CITIZENSHIP IN THE
HISTORY THAT SET OUT
TO DESTROY ITS OWN SELF

& CAN LIVE ONLY IN
ANTIHISTORIC COMPANIONSHIP
WITH THE ESSENTIALS OF
LIVES THAT RECOGNIZE
EACH OTHER & THE WATER
THEY DRINK TOGETHER

& MUST BE iF THEY
WANT TO BE & MUST
CHERiSH THEiR NECESSiTY
& MUST MUCH MORE
iF iNDEED THEY CAN BE
& WANT TO BE
A NECESSiTY

& THE HUMANS ARE LIKE VERMIN
AS VERMIN IS TO THEM

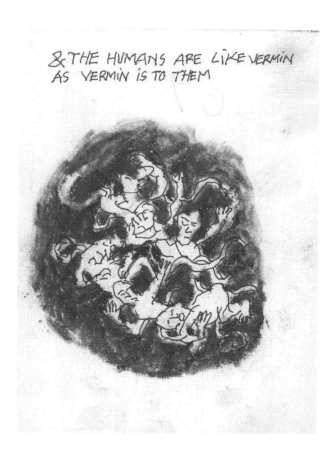

AND THE DEBRIS THAT
THE MACHINES WHICH
ARE THE SKY'S MACHINES
THROWS AT   THEM
BURNS THEIR   CITIES

AND THE OCEAN CHEATS
THEM FIRST PROMISES THEM
THE DISTANCE THEY NEED
THEN EMBRACES THEM
THEN ROCKS THEM TO&FRO
&THEN SMASHES THEM
AGAINST THE ROCKS

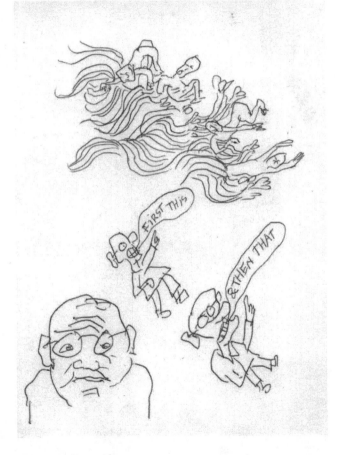

YOU WHO CAN GO, GO & YOU
NOT & YOU NOT & OTHERS ALSO
NOT, WOMEN & CHILDREN NOT
EXCEPTED YOU CAN'T JUST PROCEED
THIS MUST BE ORDERLY YOU MUST
COMPLY WITH THE RULES OF
SPECIAL BEHAVIOR AS REQUIRED
FOR SUCH OCCASIONS

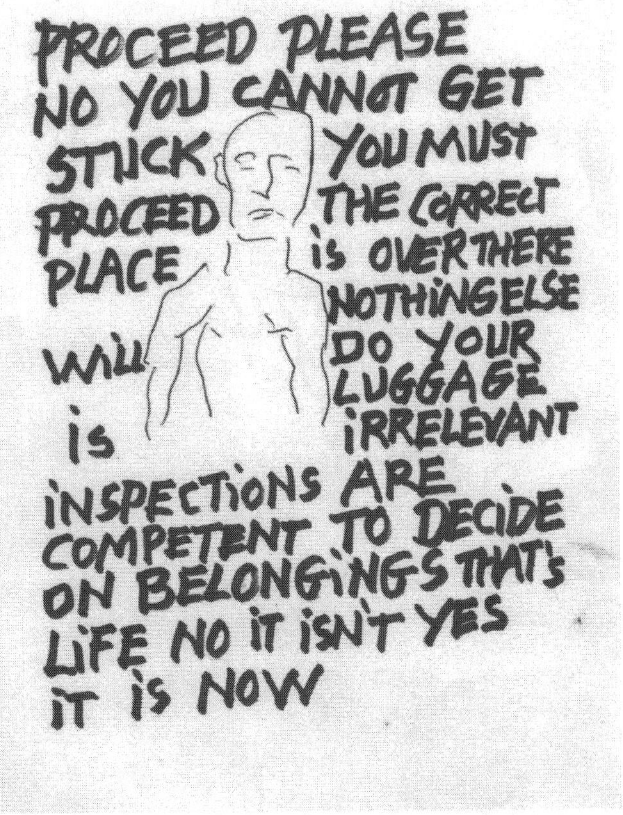

PROCEED PLEASE
NO YOU CANNOT GET
STUCK   YOU MUST
PROCEED   THE CORRECT
PLACE   is OVER THERE
               NOTHING ELSE
WILL   DO YOUR
               LUGGAGE
  is   iRRELEVANT
iNSPECTiONS ARE
COMPETENT TO DECIDE
ON BELONGINGS THAT'S
LiFE NO iT iSN'T YES
iT is NOW

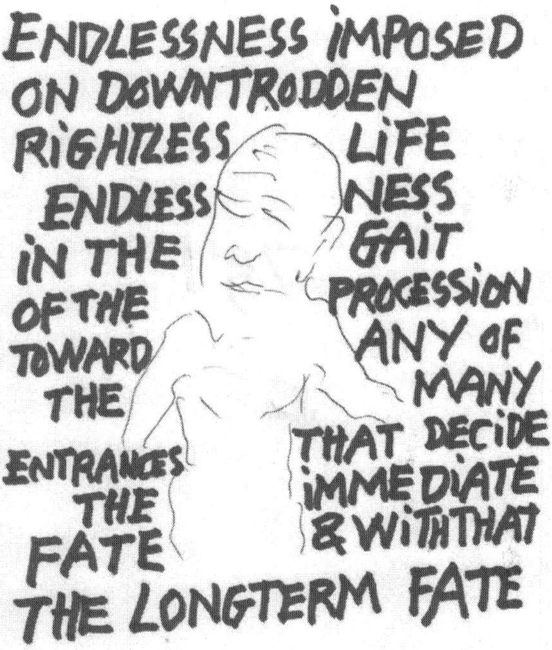

ENDLESSNESS IMPOSED
ON DOWNTRODDEN
RIGHTLESS   LIFE
   ENDLESS   NESS
   IN THE   GAIT
   OFTHE   PROCESSION
   TOWARD   ANY OF
     THE   MANY
 ENTRANCES   THAT DECIDE
    THE   IMMEDIATE
   FATE   & WITH THAT
 THE LONGTERM FATE

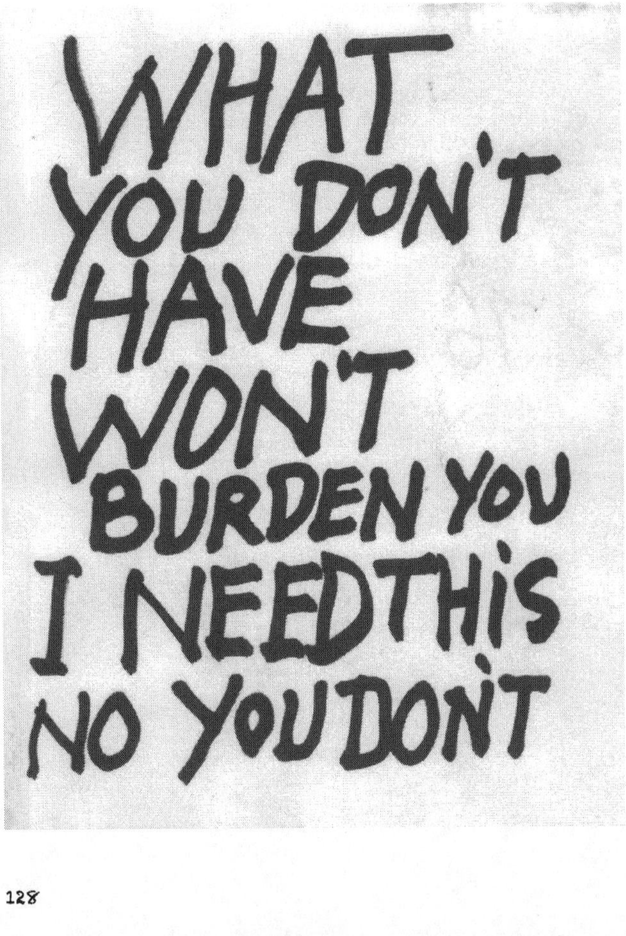

WHAT
YOU DON'T
HAVE
WON'T
BURDEN YOU
I NEEDTHIS
NO YOU DON'T

FATES USED TO BE
AVAILABLE BUT CAN
NO LONGE   R BE
PURCH   ASED
THERE   ARE
    TOO   MANY
THEY SIT   DULL
&GREY   IN
THE   DRIZZLE
THAT THE WEATHER
PROVIDES IN
COLLABORATION WITH
THE AUTHORITIES

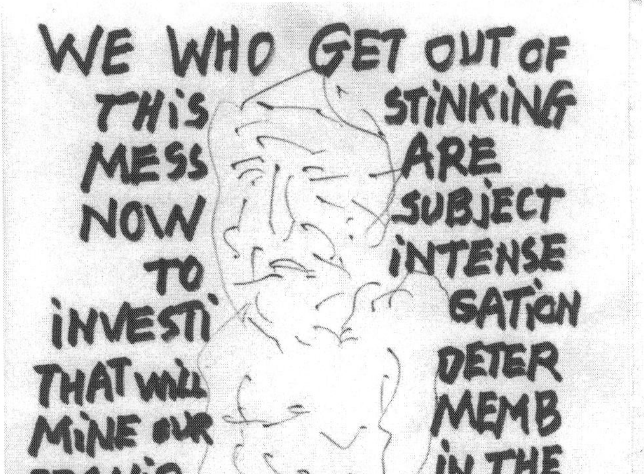

WE WHO GET OUT OF
THIS STINKING
MESS ARE
NOW SUBJECT
TO INTENSE
INVESTI GATION
THAT WILL DETER
MINE OUR MEMB
ERSHIP IN THE

HUMAN
RACE

THE LOVELY EXCESSES OF
PITY SOCKS   COFFEES
COOKIES   BLANKETS
    &   BADLY NEEDED
PILLS   OVERWHELM
THE   STINKERS
    &   WAITERS
WHO   NEED SO 
MUCH MORE & FALL ON
THEIR KNEES FOR SO MUCH
LESS. EVEN GRANDMAS WHO
ARE EXACTLY LIKE OUR OWN
GRANDMAS WON'T SUCCEED
TO GET THE CRUCIAL PETITION
SIGNED SUCCESSFULLY

NO CHILD
DIVINITY
CAN BRIBE
THE
FACILITATOR

THERE ARE MANY WHO

TRY & WANT & ARE SERIOUS
WHO SEE THE INEQUALITY &
SHAME & CRIME THAT EFFECT
ALL & DEGRADE EVERYBODY
THOSE WHOSE BODIES ARE
STILL HAPPY BUT CAN'T
SHARE THEIR HAPPY LEGS
WITH THE MAIMED THOSE
WHOSE MIND INVENTS SOLUTIONS
THAT THE INCAPACITATED
REALITY CAN'T PRODUCE
THOSE WHO ARE JAILED BY THE
COMMON LIFE JAIL

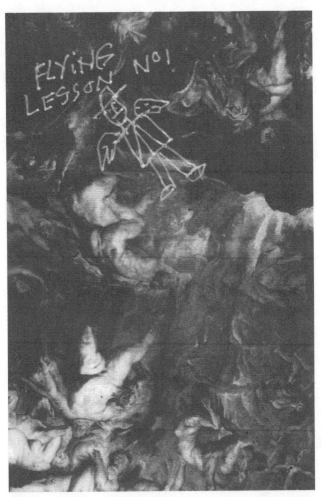

MASSES

MASSES ARE ADDRESSED
& THEN UTILIZED BY POLITICS
TILL THEIR POPULATION
POTENTIAL IS MADE
CLEAR TO THEM

MASSES ARE
SUNSETS BEFORE
THE POPULATION MOON
RISES

MASSES CROWD UP
TO CREATE LIFE INITIATION
DENSITY

HORIZONTAL MASSES ON THEIR WAY TO BECOME POPULATION

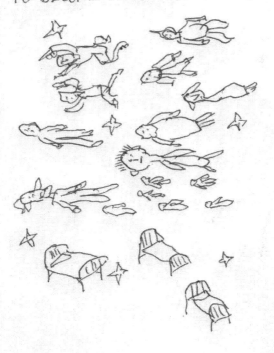

FRAGMENTS OF MASSES ON THEIR
WAY TO BECOME POPULATION

DESIROUS MASS

UNCHECKED MASSES

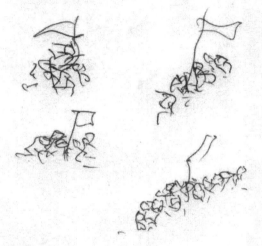

EXTINCT MASSES

CONDENSED MASS

$\frac{1}{2}$ MASS

FALLEN MASS

ELEMENTS OF MASS

MASS DIRECTIVE

ILLEGITIMATE MASSES NOT READY TO BECOME POPULATION

asylum seekers

All countries	250
Italy	140
France	110
Greece	100
Ireland	70
United Kingdom	60

Note: "Europe" consists of the EU-28, Norway and Switzerland.
Numbers rounded to nearest 10. Limited to countries with 50 or
more asylum seekers per 100,000 in country's population.

Source: Pew Research Center analysis of Eurostat data, accessed
June 22, 2016.

"Number of Refugees to Europe Surges to Record 1.3 Million in
2015"

PEW RESEARCH CENTER

the total European rate. By contrast, France
total population in 2015 and the UK had only 60

earch.org

Europe's asylum seekers did not equally disperse across countries

Number of first-time asylum applications in 2015 per 100,000 people in the country's population

Hungary	1,770
Sweden	1,600
Austria	1,000
Norway	590
Finland	590
Germany	540
Switzerland	460
Luxembourg	420
Malta	390
Denmark	370
Belgium	350
Bulgaria	280
Netherlands	250

:urope Sur~~ges~~ ~~to~~
5

en asylum applications since 1985

, the 28 member states of the European Union,
ie previous high water mark of roughly 700,000
1 and the collapse of the Soviet Union,
a from Eurostat, the European Union's

; to record 1.3 million in 2015

intries, Norway and Switzerland, 1985 to 2015

1,325,000
▼

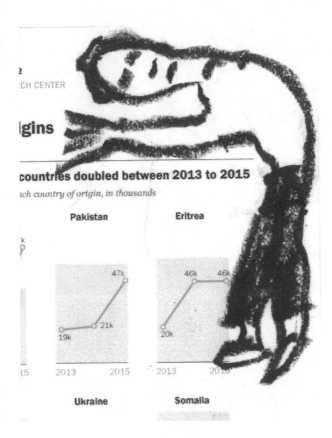

gins

countries doubled between 2013 to 2015

ich country of origin, in thousands

Pakistan

47k

19k   21k

2013   2015

Eritrea

46k   46k

20k

2013   20

k

15

Ukraine   **Somalia**

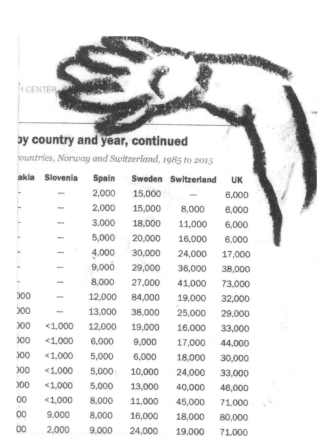

by country and year, continued

countries, Norway and Switzerland, 1985 to 2015

akia	Slovenia	Spain	Sweden	Switzerland	UK
-	—	2,000	15,000	—	6,000
-	—	2,000	15,000	8,000	6,000
-	—	3,000	18,000	11,000	6,000
-	—	5,000	20,000	16,000	6,000
-	—	4,000	30,000	24,000	17,000
-	—	9,000	29,000	36,000	38,000
-	—	8,000	27,000	41,000	73,000
)00	—	12,000	84,000	19,000	32,000
)00	—	13,000	38,000	25,000	29,000
)00	<1,000	12,000	19,000	16,000	33,000
)00	<1,000	6,000	9,000	17,000	44,000
)00	<1,000	5,000	6,000	18,000	30,000
)00	<1,000	5,000	10,000	24,000	33,000
)00	<1,000	5,000	13,000	40,000	46,000
00	<1,000	8,000	11,000	45,000	71,000
00	9,000	8,000	16,000	18,000	80,000
00	2,000	9,000	24,000	19,000	71,000

Number of asylum applications to Europe

Annual number of asylum applications received by EU-28

	Norway	Poland	Portugal	Romania	Slov
1985	<1,000	—	<1,000	—	
1986	3,000	—	<1,000	—	
1987	9,000	—	<1,000	—	
1988	7,000	—	<1,000	—	
1989	4,000	—	<1,000	—	
1990	4,000	—	<1,000	—	
1991	5,000	—	<1,000	<1,000	
1992	5,000	—	<1,000	<1,000	<1,
1993	13,000	—	2,000	<1,000	<1,
1994	3,000	<1,000	<1,000	<1,000	<1,
1995	1,000	<1,000	<1,000	<1,000	<1,
1996	2,000	<1,000	<1,000	<1,000	<1,
1997	2,000	4,000	<1,000	1,000	<1,
1998	8,000	3,000	<1,000	1,000	<1,
1999	10,000	3,000	<1,000	2,000	1,0
2000	11,000	5,000	<1,000	1,000	2,0
2001	15,000	4,000	<1,000	2,000	8,0

2002	17,000	5,000	<1,000	<1,000	10,0
2003	16,000	7,000	<1,000	<1,000	10,0
2004	8,000	8,000	<1,000	<1,000	11,0
2005	5,000	5,000	<1,000	<1,000	4,0(
2006	5,000	4,000	<1,000	<1,000	3,0(
2007	—	7,000	<1,000	<1,000	3,0(
2008	14,000	7,000	<1,000	—	—
2009	17,000	10,000	<1,000	—	—
2010	9,000	4,000	<1,000	—	<1,0
2011	9,000	5,000	<1,000	2,000	<1,0
2012	9,000	9,000	<1,000	2,000	<1,0
2013	11,000	14,000	<1,000	1,000	<1,0
2014	11,000	6,000	<1,000	2,000	<1,0
2015	31,000	10,000	<1,000	1,000	<1,0

Note: "Europe" consis... the EU... rway and Switzerland. Asylum s...
for asylum applic... s since... first time applicants ar...
countries. Dat... sy... pp... some countries in ...

Source: Pew... nter analysis of Eur... ta, accessed June ...

"Number of ... Europe Surges to Re... 3 Million in 2015"

PEW RESE... CH CENTER

www.pewres...

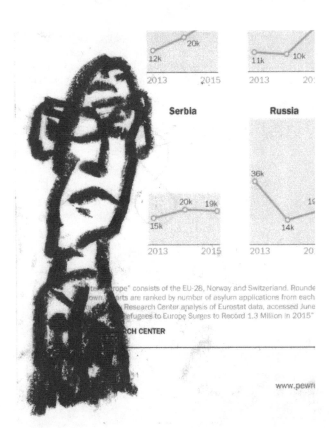

20k		
12k	11k	10k
2013	2015	2013	20:

Serbia

Russia

20k	19k	36k
15k		
2013	2015	2013	20:

14k

19

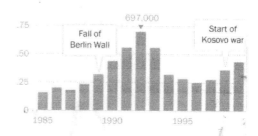

697,000

.75

Fall of
Berlin Wall

.50

Start of
Kosovo war

.25

0

1985   1990   1995

Note: "Europe" consists of the EU-28, Norway and Switzerland. Asylum r
for asylum applications since 2008 are based on first-time applicants a
countries. See methodology for more details. Data on asylum applicatio
of countries with missing data. All countries that are part of the EU toda
part of the European Union in earlier years. Rounded to nearest thousar

Source: Pew Research Center analysis of Eurostat data, accessed June

"Number of Refugees to Europe Surges to Record 1.3 Million in 2015"

PEW RESEARCH CENTER

www.pewre

received the highest number of asylum applications in 2015. Meanwhile, France (71,000) and the UK (39,000) received roughly the same number of applications in 2015 as in years just prior to the refugee surge in 2015.

Refugees did not disperse equally across Europe, with some countries taking in more asylum seekers than the European average. In 2015, the EU-28, Norway and Switzerland as a whole had 250 asylum applicants per 100,000 residents. By comparison, Hungary had 1,770 applicants per 100,000 people (the highest of any country) and Sweden had 1,600 applicants per 100,000 people. Meanwhile, Germany had 540 applicants per 100,000 people, still well abov had only 110 applicants per 100,000 people in its asylum seekers per 100,000 people.

Today, Eastern European countries like Kosovo and Albania still contribute to the overall flow of asylum seekers into the EU, Norway and Switzerland, but about half of refugees in 2015 trace their origins to just three countries: Syria, Afghanistan and Iraq. Conflicts, both fresh and long-standing, in each of these states have led to the displacement of hundreds of thousands of people. Some have been displaced within their homelands; others have sought refuge in neighboring countries; and still others have made the often perilous journey to Europe (and elsewhere) to seek asylum.

Since 2012, Germany has been the primary destination country for asylum seekers in Europe, receiving 442,000 asylum applications in 2015 alone. Following Germany, Hungary (174,000 applications) and Sweden (156,000)

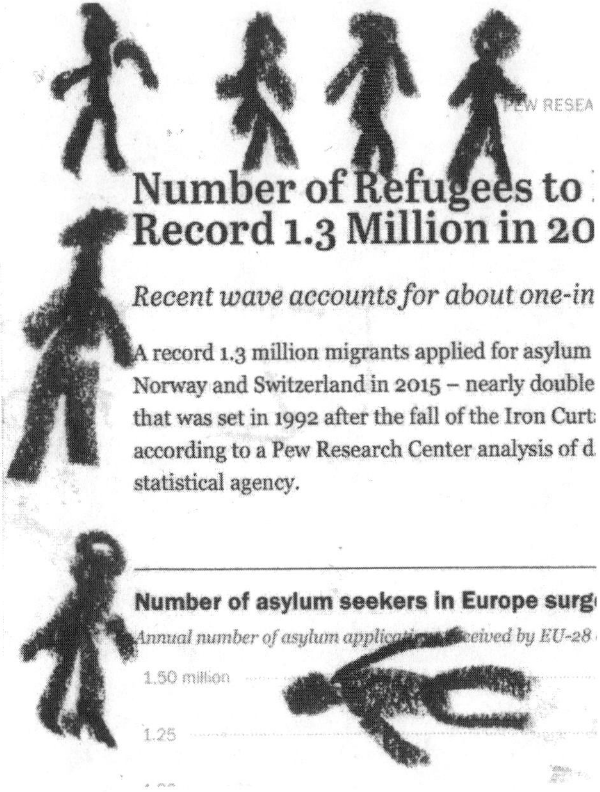

Number of Refugees to Record 1.3 Million in 20

Recent wave accounts for about one-in

A record 1.3 million migrants applied for asylum
Norway and Switzerland in 2015 – nearly double
that was set in 1992 after the fall of the Iron Curt
according to a Pew Research Center analysis of d
statistical agency.

Number of asylum seekers in Europe surg

Annual number of asylum applica   ceived by EU-28

1.50 million

1.25

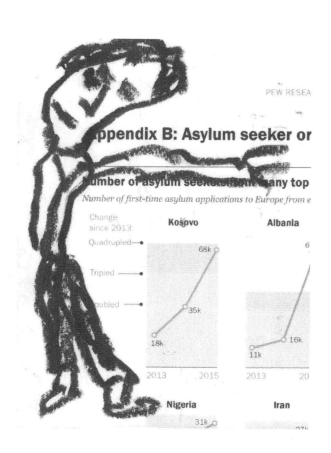

ppendix B: Asylum seeker or

umber of asylum seeke... any top

Number of first-time asylum applications to Europe from e

Change
since 2013:

Quadrupled →

Tripled →

ubled →

Kosovo

68k

35k

18k

2013   2015

Albania

6

16k

11k

2013   20

Nigeria

31k

Iran

Bangladesh   Gambia

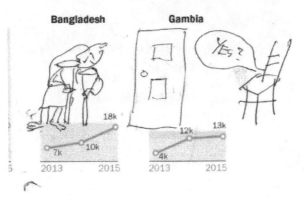

to nearest thousand. Only leading countries of origin in 2015 are
ountry in 2015.
!2, 2016.

search.org

)0	<1,000	6,000	33,000	24,000	103,000
)0	1,000	6,000	31,000	20,000	60,000
)0	1,000	5,000	23,000	13,000	41,000
0	2,000	5,000	18,000	9,000	31,000
0	<1,000	5,000	24,000	9,000	28,000
0	<1,000	7,000	36,000	10,000	28,000
	<1,000	—	24,000	15,000	31,000
	<1,000	—	24,000	14,000	31,000
)0	<1,000	3,000	32,000	14,000	23,000
)0	<1,000	3,000	30,000	19,000	26,000
)0	<1,000	2,000	44,000	26,000	28,000
)0	<1,000	4,000	54,000	19,000	30,000
)0	<1,000	5,000	75,000	22,000	32,000
)0	<1,000	15,000	156,000	38,000	39,000

eeker definitions varied by European country prior to 2008. Numbers
d do not include appeals or transfer of applications between
ome years, indicated by '—'. Rounded to nearest thousand.

2, 2016.

efugees to
es to Record
2015

ne-in-ten asylum applications

at informs the public about the issues, attitudes
s not take policy positions. The Center conducts
tent analysis and other data-driven social
; journalism and media; internet, science and
ds; global attitudes and trends; and U.S. social
s are available at www.pewresearch.org. Pew
able Trusts, its primary funder.

PewResearch Center

FOR RELEASE AUGUST 2, 2016

Number of R
Europe Surg
1.3 Million in

Recent wave accounts for about (

CENTER

...tries

...pe's leading destination

...across Europe

Table of Contents

RESEAR

Yugoslavia and USSR. (See detailed chart in Appe

besides Syria, Afghanistan and Iraq.)

Not all asylum seekers are allowed to stay i

The success rate for asylum seekers varies dramaticall

nearly all asylum seekers from Syria (97%) whose appl

the first decision round. The great majority of Eritreans

between 60% and 70% of Afghani, Iranian and Somalia

other leading nationalities of asylum seekers in Europe

Meanwhile, less than 5% of asylum cases from other E

Serbia were given positive decisions in 2015.

Once an application and all appeals for asylum are der

force or through voluntary means. These returns, howe

seekers fall below the radar and illegally remain in Eurc

worsening security in the origin country or for other hun

Germany is leading destination; UK, I

Hungary received the second largest number of a
received 174,000 asylum applications or about 1!

Sweden received the third highest number of asy
asylum seekers has grown to about 10% or more
record 156,000 applicants in 2015. Sweden alon
the UK combined. Sweden was also the most por
asylum seekers under age 18, receiving 35,000 a

Germany again the leading destination of

Number of asylum applications in Europe by year and ap

1.50 million

1.25

1.00

All other 259,000

1. Asylum seeker origins: A rap

In 2015, a record 1.3 million individuals applied fo
Switzerland. This was more than a twofold
increase from 2014, when nearly 600,000
people applied for asylum. This dramatic rise in
asylum applications followed a relatively stable
period of about roughly 200,000 applicants
each year between 2005 and 2010 and around
300,000 annual applicants in 2011 and 2012.

The leading country of citizenship for Europe's
asylum applicants in 2015 was Syria, which
accounted for 378,000 asylum seekers, or 29%
of all applicants. Second was Afghanistan, with
193,000 asylum seekers in 2015. Well over half
(53%) of all asylum seekers in 2015 held
citizenship from one of these countries or Iraq.

A mixed group of source countries represent the remaining leading points of origin for asylum seekers in Europe during 2015. Kosovo and Albania were each the country of origin of about 5% of asylum seekers. In fact, Europe received about the same number of asylum applications from Kosovo and Albania combined as from Iraq in 2015. Slightly fewer than 50,000 asylum seekers had Pakistani or Eritrean citizenship in 2015. Asylum applicants from Iran, several sub-Saharan countries like Nigeria, Somalia and Gambia, as well as European countries such as Ukraine, Serbia and Russia rounded out the leading countries of citizenship for Europe's asylum

Germany received an unprecedented 442,000 indivi

the highest annual number ever received by a Europ

applicants to Germany alone accounted for about on

Germany has long been a primary destination for as

received nearly half of Europe's annual asylum appli

has received at least 3.6 million asylum applications

applications in Europe over the period.

France and the UK were once leading destinations o

2010, France was the leading destination of asylum

leading destination for four years. However, in 201?

applicants than Germany, Hungary or Sweden. The

last year, while France received 71,000 applications

---

[2] The refugee issue was highly debated in the UK's June vote to leave the
from other EU countries. Overall, about a third of the UK's immigrants (2.
being Poland (700,000), Ireland (500,000) and Germany (320,000).

the three leading origin
countries: Syria, Afghanistan
and Iraq.

Note: "Europe" cons
thousand.

Source: Pew Researc

"Number of Refugees

PEW RESEARCH CEN

Refugees from Syria
numbered 378,000 in 2015,
accounting for 29% of all of
Europe's asylum seekers – the
highest share of any nation. This was up from 12
drive the recent surge in asylum applications. An
were from other relatively new origin countries, i
23,000 in 2013 and 39,000 in 2014) and another
15,000 in 2014).

Some of the origins of Europe's asylum seekers i
migrants. Nearly one-in-five asylum seekers in 2
the EU, Norway and Switzerland, including asylu
35,000 in 2014), Albania (67,000 in 2015, up fro
up from 14,000 in 2014), regions that had once s

www.pewr

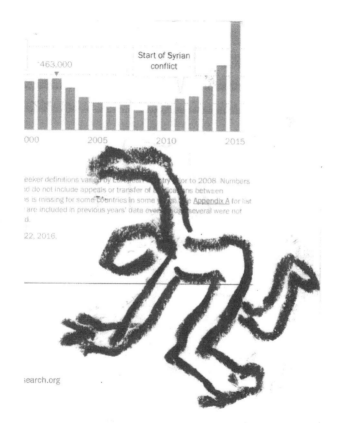

463,000

Start of Syrian
conflict

000   2005   2010   2015

eeker definitions vary by country prior to 2008. Numbers
d do not include appeals or transfer of applications between
is is missing for some countries in some years. See Appendix A for list
are included in previous years' data even though several were not
d.

22, 2016.

search.org

received more than a quarter of annual asylum s quarter or more of Europe's annual asylum app destination.

Germany is the largest recipient of a

When summed together for all years between 1985 and 2015, nearly one-third (more than 3.6 million) of Europe's asylum applications were registered in Germany. And since 1985, the UK and France each received about one-in-ten (or more than 1 million) of Europe's asylum applications.

Countries with smaller resident populations such as Sweden, the Netherlands, Switzerland and Belgium also each received hundreds of thousands of asylum applications between 1985 and 2015.

The EU, Norway and Switzerland saw large increases of asylum seekers in 2014 from some of the largest countries of origin in 2013 and again for the same countries between 2014 and 2015, when the latest wave of asylum seekers reached Europe. For several leading source countries, the volume of asylum applications doubled in 2014 (from 2013) and doubled again for many countries in 2015 (from 2014).

Syria had the greatest annual asylum applicant increase between 2013 and 2015, with about 49,000 asylum seekers in 2013, 125,000 in 2014 and 378,000 in 2015.

But it was Ukraine, Iraq and Afghanistan that saw the greatest annual *percentage* increases between 2013 and 2015 among the top 15 source countries of asylum seekers in 2015.

kers in Europe. France and the UK never had a
ations when they were the leading countries of

ylum applications since 1985

About one-third of asylum applications since 1985 were filed in Germany

Leading 15 countries of application of all Europe asylum applications between 1985 and 2015

	Total	% of all asylum applicants
Germany	3,654,000	12
France	1,227,000	11
UK	1,151,000	10
Sweden	987,000	9
Netherlands	658,000	5
Switzerland	631,000	5
Belgium	517,000	4
Austria	498,000	4

the EU 28, Norway and Switzerland. Rounded to nearest

ter analysis of Eur... ... accessed June ... ... 16.

rope Surges to Record 1... Million in 2015"

_____

)0 in 2014 and 49,000 in 2013, helping to

litional quarter of asylum seekers in 2015

iding 193,000 from Afghanistan (up from

7,000 from Iraq (up from 9,000 in 2013 and

15 were regions that have sent past waves of

(17%) came from European countries outside

eekers from Kosovo (68,000 in 2015, up from

5,000 in 2014) and Ukraine (21,000 in 2015,

igrants when they were a part of the former

ch.org

Number of all asylum applications grew by about half in 2014 and more than doubled in 2015

Citizenship of first-time asylum applicants in Europe

	2013	2014	2015
Syria	49,000	125,000	378,000
Afghanistan	23,000	39,000	193,000
Iraq	9,000	15,000	127,000
Kosovo	15,000	35,000	68,000
Albania	11,000	16,000	67,000
Pakistan	19,000	21,000	47,000
Eritrea	20,000	46,000	46,000
Nigeria	12,000	20,000	31,000
Iran	11,000	10,000	27,000
Somalia	18,000	16,000	21,000
Ukraine	1,000	14,000	21,000
Serbia	15,000	20,000	19,000
Russia	36,000	14,000	19,000
Bangladesh	7,000	10,000	18,000
Gambia	4,000	12,000	13,000

d rise for most countries

asylum in the European Union, Norway and

Syrians, Afghans, Iraqis were over half of all Europe's asylum seekers in 2015

Citizenship of first-time asylum applicants in Europe, 2015

	Total	% of all asylum applications
Syria	378,000	29
Afghanistan	193,000	15
Iraq	127,000	10
Kosovo	68,000	5
Albania	67,000	5
Pakistan	47,000	4
Eritrea	46,000	3
Nigeria	31,000	2
Iran	27,000	2
Somalia	21,000	2
Ukraine	21,000	2
Serbia	19,000	1

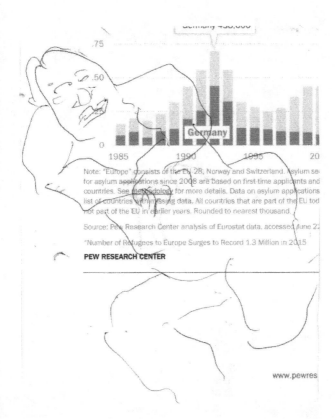

Germany 430,000

.75

.50

0

1985   1990   1995   20

Note: "Europe" consists of the EU-28, Norway and Switzerland. Asylum se
for asylum applications since 2008 are based on first-time applicants and
countries. See methodology for more details. Data on asylum applications
list of countries with missing data. All countries that are part of the EU tod
not part of the EU in earlier years. Rounded to nearest thousand.

Source: Pew Research Center analysis of Eurostat data, accessed June 22

"Number of Refugees to Europe Surges to Record 1.3 Million in 2015

PEW RESEARCH CENTER

www.pewres

Rapid increase in the number of asylu European countries alike between 20

In 2014, nearly 600,000 asylum applications were filed in the EU, Norway and Switzerland, a 47% increase over the more than 400,000 applications filed in 2013. In 2015, the number of asylum applications grew again, this time more than doubling 2014's record to reach about 1.3 million (a 122% increase). The overall increase from 2013 to 2014 and again between 2014 and 2015 was reflected in the trajectory of new asylum seekers arriving from each of

Number of as Iraq more tha

Number of first-ti origin, in thousan

Change
since 2013:

Quadrupled →

Tripled →

Doubled →

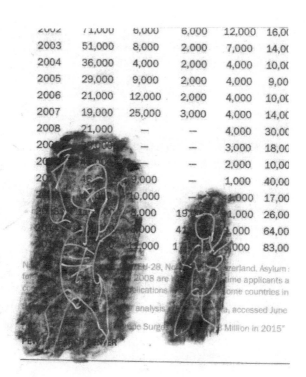

2002	71,000	6,000	6,000	12,000	16,0(
2003	51,000	8,000	2,000	7,000	14,0(
2004	36,000	4,000	2,000	4,000	10,0(
2005	29,000	9,000	2,000	4,000	9,00
2006	21,000	12,000	2,000	4,000	10,0(
2007	19,000	25,000	3,000	4,000	14,0(
2008	21,000	—	—	4,000	30,0(
200	,000	—	—	3,000	18,0(
20			—	2,000	10,0(
20		9,000	—	1,000	40,00
		10,000	—	,000	17,00
		,000	19	,000	26,00
	,000	42	,000	64,00
	,000	17	000	83,00

N... EU-28, No... ...zerland. Asylum :
fo... 2008 are ...ime applicants a
C... ...lications ...ome countries in

...analysis ...a, accessed June

...de Surge... ...Million in 2015"

7,000	7,000	<1,000	3,000	31,000
9,000	10,000	<1,000	3,000	39,000
18,000	13,000	<1,000	2,000	47,000
8,000	6,000	<1,000	3,000	51,000
11,000	4,000	<1,000	3,000	60,000
5,000	3,000	<1,000	4,000	59,000
4,000	2,000	<1,000	,000	50,000
3,000	2,000	<1,00	,000	31,000
2,000	2,000	<1,0	0	29,000
1,000	2,000	<1		—
<1,000	4,000	<1		42,000
<1,000	5,000	<1		48,000
<1,000	4,000			52,000
<1,000	6,000			54,000
<1,000	7,000			
<1,000	15,000		0	
1,000	21,00		00	

eker definitions var... ...prior to 20...
i do not include app... ...cations be...
me years, indicate... ...arest thous...

, 2016.

earch.org

Number of asylum applications to Europe

Annual number of asylum applications received by EU-28

	Germany	Greece	Hungary	Ireland	Ital
1985	74,000	1,000	—	—	5,0(
1986	100,000	4,000	—	—	7,0(
1987	57,000	6,000	—	<1,000	11,0
1988	103,000	9,000	—	<1,000	1,0(
1989	121,000	7,000	—	<1,000	2,0(
1990	193,000	4,000	—	<1,000	4,0(
1991	256,000	3,000	—	<1,000	24,0(
1992	438,000	2,000	—	<1,000	3,0(
1993	323,000	<1,000	—	<1,000	1,0(
1994	127,000	1,000	—	<1,000	2,0(
1995	128,000	1,000	—	<1,000	2,0(
1996	117,000	2,000	1,000	1,000	<1,0(
1997	104,000	4,000	—	4,000	2,0(
1998	99,000	3,000	7,000	5,000	13,0(
1999	95,000	2,000	12,000	8,000	18,0
2000	79,000	3,000	8,000	11,000	15,0
2001	88,000	6,000	10,000	10,000	17,0

Appendix A: Asylum applicati

Number of asylum applications to Europ

Annual number of asylum applications received by EU-2

	Austria	Belgium	Bulgaria	Croatia	Cypr
1985	7,000	5,000	—	—	—
1986	9,000	8,000	—	—	—
1987	11,000	6,000	—	—	—
1988	16,000	5,000	—	—	—
1989	22,000	8,000	—	—	—
1990	23,000	13,000	—	—	—
1991	27,000	15,000	—	—	—
1992	16,000	18,000	—	—	—
1993	5,000	27,000	—	—	—
1994	5,000	14,000	—	—	—
1995	6,000	11,000	—	—	—
1996	7,000	12,000	—	—	—
1997	7,000	12,000	<1,000	—	—
1998	14,000	22,000	<1,000	—	<1,0

s 1985 through 2015

y country

untries, Nor

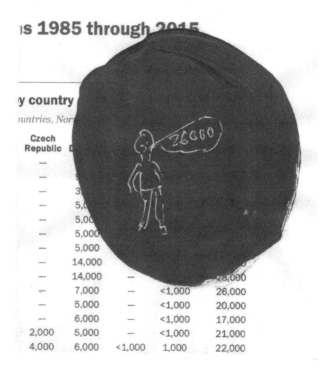

Czech Republic	D			
—				
—	9			
—	3			
—	5,0			
—	5,00			
—	5,000			
—	5,000			
—	14,000			
—	14,000			28,000
—	7,000	—	<1,000	26,000
—	5,000	—	<1,000	20,000
—	6,000	—	<1,000	17,000
2,000	5,000	—	<1,000	21,000
4,000	6,000	<1,000	1,000	22,000

<u>dix B</u> noting the increase in origin countries

Europe
by country
ations wer
and Iraqis
n asylum
had posi
ropean

ed, the sta
er, are not
pe. Others ha
anitarian reason

rance receive fewer asylum seekers

dual first-time asylum applications in 2015 –
ean country over the past 30 years. Asylum
e-third of Europe's 2015 asylum seekers.

ylum seekers. In the late 1980s and 1990s, it
cations. And over the past 30 years, Germany
, or nearly one-third (32%) of all asylum

f Europe's a
seekers fo
, both th
UK rec

2

uropean
million or

rch.org

R CENTER

m seekers from non-European and
13 and 2015

ylum seekers from Syri... ...n and
n quadrupled betw...

ne asylum applicatio...
s

Syria

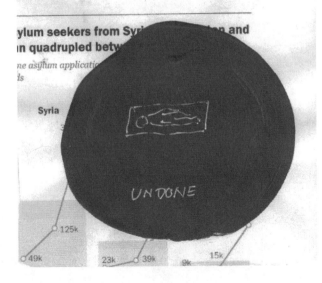

125k

49k   23k   39k   9k   15k

ussia	19,000	1
angladesh	18,000	1
ambia	13,000	1
ther	230,000	17
)TAL	1,325,000	100

ote: "Europe" consists of t   witzerland. Only
gin countries with 1
nrounded) show
ercentages calc
ateless appli

ource: Pew
ne 22, 2

lumbe
)15"

EW RE

seek

ch.org

All other European destination countries

2005   2015

ker definitions varied
do not include app
are missing for
y are included

, 2016.

arch.org

UNDEFINED

| Other | 151,000 | 182,000 | 230,000 |
| TOTAL | 405,000 | 596,000 | 1,325,000 |

Note: "Europe" consists of the EU-28, Norway and Switzerland. Only origin countries with 1% or more of total asylum applicants (unrounded) in 2015 shown. Numbers rounded to nearest thousand. Percentages calculated from unrounded numbers. Sorted by total number of asylum seekers in 2015.

Source: Pew Research Center a███████████at data, accessed June 22, 2016.

"Number of Refug██████████████████
2015"

PEW RESE██

earch.org

Italy	490,000	4
Hungary	289,000	2
Norway	266,000	2
Denmark	210,000	2
Spain	182,000	2
Greece	169,000	1
Poland	123,000	1
Other	525,000	5
TOTAL	11,576,0	00

Notes: "Europe" consists
Rounded to nearest
unrounded num
applicants. As
harmonization
methodolog
Appendix

Source:
June 2

"Num
2015"

PEW R

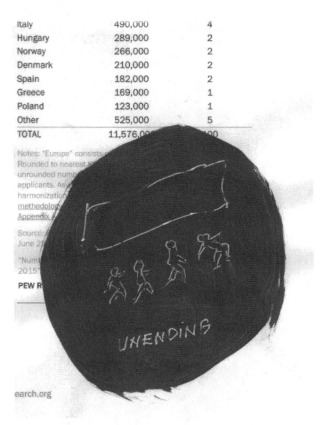

UNENDING

earch.org

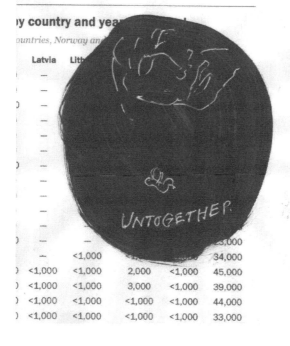

y country and yea

ountries, Norway an

	Latvia	Lith			
	—				
	—				
)	—				
	—				
)	—				
	—				
	—				
	—				
	—				
)	—	—			3,000
	—	<1,000			34,000
)	<1,000	<1,000	2,000	<1,000	45,000
)	<1,000	<1,000	3,000	<1,000	39,000
)	<1,000	<1,000	<1,000	<1,000	44,000
)	<1,000	<1,000	<1,000	<1,000	33,000

1999	20,000	36,000	1,000	—	<1,000
2000	18,000	43,000	2,000	—	<1,000
2001	30,000	25,000	2,000	—	2,000
2002	39,000	19,000	3,000	—	<1,000
2003	32,000	14,000	1,000	—	4,000
2004	25,000	12,000	<1,000	—	10,000
2005	22,000	13,000	<1,000	—	8,000
2006	13,000	9,000	<1,000	—	5,000
2007	12,000	12,000	<1,000	—	7,000
2008	—	11,000			4,000
2009	—			—	3,000
2010				—	3,000
2011				—	2,000
2012				—	2,000
2013				,000	1,000
201				,000	1,000
20				,000	2,000

COMING

Note: [...] itzerland. Asylum [...] for asy[...] t-time applicants a countries [...] r some countries in

Source: Pew Re[...] et data, accessed June

"Number of Refugees to [...] ecord 1.3 Million in 2015"

PEW RESEARCH CENTER

ylum applicants in 2015. In all, Hungary
6 of Europe's asylum seekers in 2015.

FLYiNG
LESSON
N°2

FLYING LESSON Nº3

CRUCIFIXION

ON THE WAY TO THE VALLEY WHERE IT WILL BE CRUCIFIED

FIRST IT FALLS BECAUSE OF REGRET

216

SOUL

CH CENTER

plicants (EUR

do/policies/as

995." Luxemb
n-europe-198

MdSRoEAlM
eName=CAN
001-EN-C

Eurostat, A
l/index.php/

European Union." Luxembourg: Eurostat,
/3433488/5285137/KS-SF-07-110-
z

2016 "Europeans fear wave of refugees will
.C.: Pew Research Center, July.

s-fear-wave-of-refugees-will-m

THE SOUL'S ORIGINAL HIGH UP POSITION

"Europe ... n." Wash... 6/05/10

"About s... rch Cente... /13/abou...

"5 facts a... er, June. /21/5-fact...

"Immigrant share of population jumps in some earch Center, June. /15/immigrant-share-of-population-jumps-in-

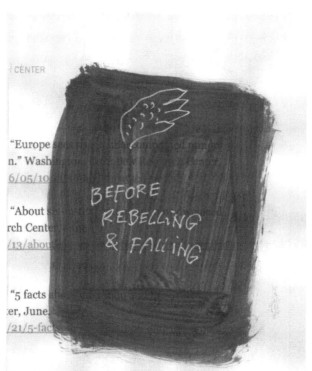

BEFORE
REBELLING
& FALLING

Wike, Richard, Bruce Stokes and Katie Simmons
mean more terrorism, fewer jobs." Washington,
http://www.pewglobal.org/2016/07/11/europea
terrorism-fewer-jobs/

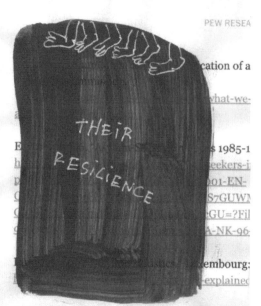

cation of a

what-we-

E   1985-1
h   eekers-i
p   001-EN-
C   S7GUW
C   GU=?Fil
9   A-NK-96-

            embourg:
            -explained

Juchno, Piotr. 2007. "Asylum applications in the
August. http://ec.europa.eu/eurostat/documents
EN.PDF/c95cc2ce-b50c-498e-95fb-cd507ef29e2

the Dublin Regulation: Asylum seekers must app
and if they do not they can be returned to the fir
applications. Most EU countries, Norway and Sw
agreement people to cross betwe

The term **cou**
report. Hi zer
country to

The term he
first appl ne
apply for th
apply is p

"Corrido a
even if m cou
Syria-Ger o Sy
Syrian rel cou
reaching

urostat, April:
1/7233417/3-20042016-AP-EN.pdf/

orld's migrants liv
p://www.p
s-migrants

d to describ

it." Washin

ticism-beyo

ponse – Me

?id=83

earch.org

H CENTER

sylum ap
have app
emale, chil
will neces
asylum se

ing confli
, the term

national bo
an country
nt, for exam
e of the EU-28

orthand for the 28 nation-states that form the
zerland, for a total of 30 countries. At the time of
of the European Union even though the country

for asylum in the first EU country they enter,
ountry they enter for the processing of their
erland are also part of the Schengen
countries without border stops

ry" are u... in ... for asy... se... ...
ching the ... untry of applica...

...ntry of ap... ...tion where an asylum seeker
...blin Regu... ...on call... for ... ... to
...enter, the ...tina... ...th... ...y
...t into Eu...pe ...

...rticular or... ...rticular... ...ory,
...tries befor... ...their final destination. The
...ans migr... ... ...hy
...tries such... ...rkey or ...reece... ...

THAT BiRTHS
THE POPULATION

bibliography and partially obscured references with overlaid handwritten text

...bout the U.S. rank in worldwide migration."
...://www.pewresearch.org/fact-
...orldwide-migrat...

...rranean death ... ...Commissioner for Refugees.
...9d94/mediter... ...

... Asylum System, Brussels, Belgium, Europe...

.../policies/asyl...

...e for asylum application (Dublin)." Brussels...

.../policies/as...

...earch.org

IS NOT POSSIBLE WITHOUT THE UNBEARABLE

Re

Co... ...Krogstad. 2016. see... ...from Afghanista... Ma... ...e/fact-tank/201

Co... ...Krogstad. 2016. fro... ...D.C.: Pew Resea ht... ...ank/2016/06 fro...

Co... ...ogstad. 2016. Ki... ...Research Cent ht... ...ink/2016/06 kin...

Connor, Philip and Jens Manuel Krogstad. 2016. European countries." Washington, D.C.: Pew Res http://www.pewresearch.org/fact-tank/2016/06

Term

The te... lums ...er...ees" and "...
throug... t...e repo... ...dividuals wh
As of 2... ...er male or
asylum...k...g ...p...n applicant...
Howeve... ...llow... ...pp...oved, th
given ... ...m

"Ref...ees" ...s both ...ic ...f people fle
in Eu...e has been a...r... (For ...atter group

"Mig...ts" ...ers t...the ...wing ...cross inter
for m... ...e ...o... ... ...e Europe
the E...ean ...on's ...a... ...e ...dered a migra
to newcomers who are citi...s ...ntries outsid

The term **"Europe"** is used in this report as a sh...
European Union (EU) as well as Norway and Swit...
the production of this report, the UK was still par...

Connor, Phillip and Gustavo López. 2016. "5 fac
Washington, D.C.: Pew Research Center, May.
tank/2016/05/18/5-facts-about-the-u-s-rank-i

2016. "Med
Nations Hig
2016/5/574

European Commission. non Europe
Commun
/what-we-

European Commission. Country responsi
Belgium /what-we-

THEY LEARN RESTLESSNESS FROM REFUGEES

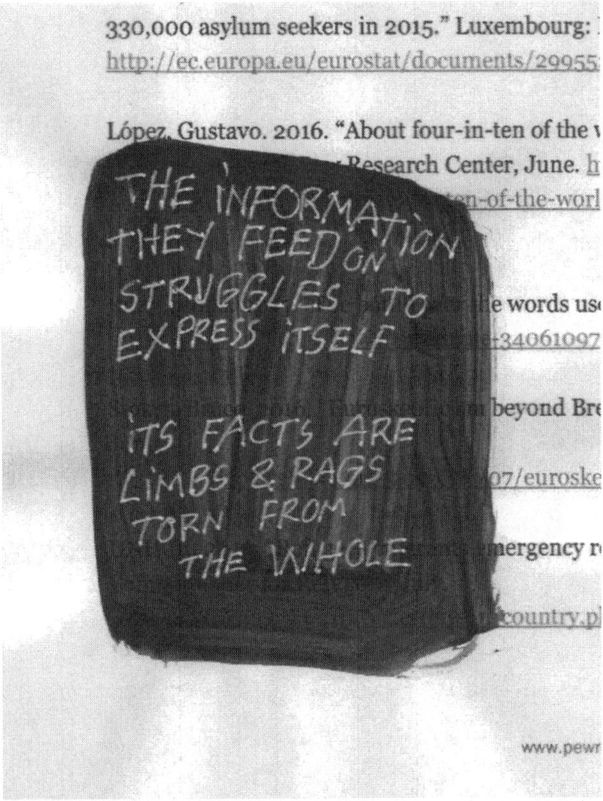

330,000 asylum seekers in 2015." Luxembourg:

http://ec.europa.eu/eurostat/documents/29955

López. Gustavo. 2016. "About four-in-ten of the v
Research Center, June. h
n-of-the-worl

e words us
34061097

beyond Bre

07/eurosk

mergency r

country.p

THE INFORMATION
THEY FEED ON
STRUGGLES TO
EXPRESS ITSELF

ITS FACTS ARE
LIMBS & RAGS
TORN FROM
THE WHOLE

About the data

asylum seeker data presented in this report are ba
EU... and then member states, Norway and Swi
Since 20... countries hav... ided Eurost
standardized definitions. S... to avoid duplicatio
(not appeal) were use... ... its analysis fo

... ...ed by Eurostat were
... ...definitions of asylum see
... ...or to 2008 a
... ... next... asylum application
... ...Eurostat revisi... ... result, data
included in this report. For more information on
see the report's methodology.

THE PROXIMITY
OF THE ONE MASSIVE
SOUL OF THE MASSES

The number of European Union member states h
1995, 2004 and 2007. Although data for some co
A), historical estimates of asylum seekers in this

Hungary and Austria, whose <u>foreign-born shares</u> r
year. By way of comparison, the foreign-born shar
1 percentage point between 2005 and 2015. (The U
<u>immigrants</u> and has historically been the world's t

Although Europe has received a large number of S
began, only about <u>one-in-ten displaced Syrians</u> wo
is internally displaced within Syria or is living as r

CAJOLES THE
SOULS INTO THEIR
DARING EXPERIMENTAL
ASSOCIATION
WITH THE MATERIALS
& ISSUES AT HAND

www.pewre

2. Asylum seeker destinations leading destination

Of the 1.3 million asylum seekers entering the European Union, Norway and Switzerland in 2015, 75% applied for asylum in just three countries: Germany, Italy and Sweden. Among these three nations, Germany received more asylum than the other two combined and retained its status as Europe's leading destination for asylum seekers, a distinction it has held since 2012.

Germany received about a third (or 442,000) of Europe's asylum applications in 2015. This was well over twice as many applicants as it received in 2014 (174,000).

THEY ARE CONSTANTLY IN UPHEAVAL

How Europe's asylum process works

When an asylum seeker travels through one of Europ
border or an airport), they can apply for asylum at the
happens, applicants are fingerprinted by authorities a
shelter as they wait for their case to be reviewed by ir

If the decision is positive, asylum applicants are deer
residency in Europe, including access to the job mark
provided health care. If the decision is negative, asyl
case reviewed again. Or, if no appeal is taken by the
citizenship or the last country they left before enterin

The European Union's 28 member states operate un
of rules and regulations for handling asylum seekers

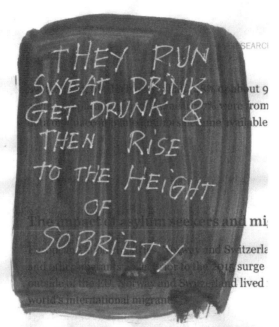

THEY RUN
SWEAT DRINK
GET DRUNK &
THEN RISE
TO THE HEIGHT
OF
SOBRIETY

% or about 9

were from

of the same available

The impact of asylum seekers and mi

way and Switzerla

prior to the 2015 surge

way and Switzerland lived

world's international migrants

Even though a record number of asylum seekers a
limited impact on the share of the overall residen
that is foreign born. That share is up only 0.3 per
to 11.3% in 2016. It has had a large impact, howev

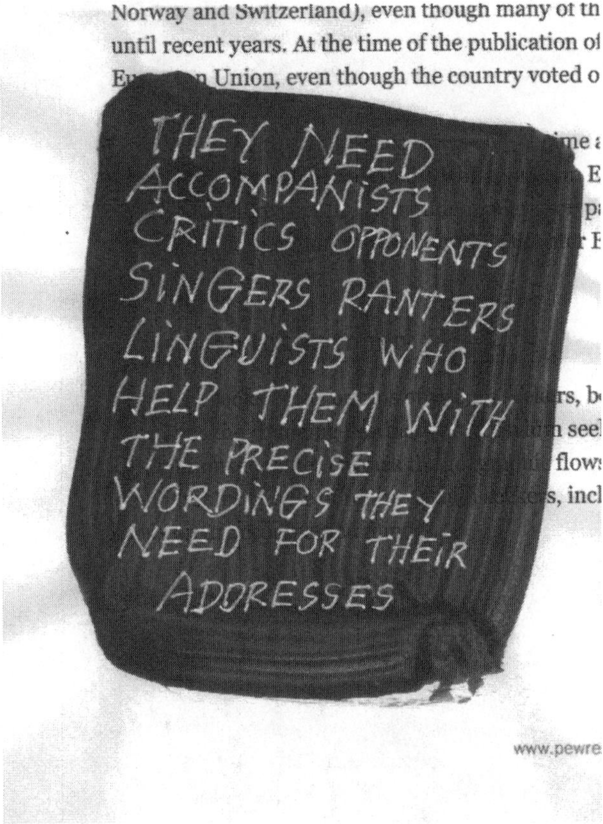

Norway and Switzerland), even though many of th
until recent years. At the time of the publication of
Eu___n Union, even though the country voted o

THEY NEED
ACCOMPANISTS
CRITICS OPPONENTS
SINGERS RANTERS
LINGUISTS WHO
HELP THEM WITH
THE PRECISE
WORDINGS THEY
NEED FOR THEIR
ADDRESSES

welcome aid (food, medicine, shelter) given to applicar

The cornerstone of the Asylum Procedures Directive is
Dublin Regulation (named after the city where the earli
[first country they]
[nother cou]
[aived this]

[ugh the fi]
[months]
[fter a neg]

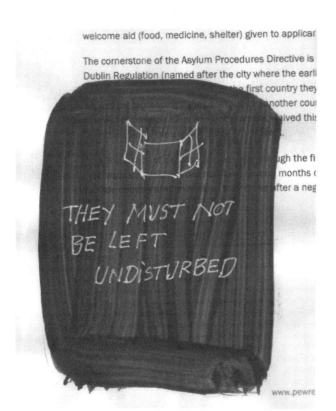

THEY MUST NOT
BE LEFT
UNDISTURBED

Asylum seekers to Europe are largely

Over half (53%) of asylum seekers to the European ___ ___ were young adul___ ___top age grou___ ___ree leading ___ Syria (50%) ___ults in 2015

___fourths (7___ ___leading or ___ ___anistan (___ ___t, asylum ___ ___bia (97% ___ ___on, were al___

THEY MUST JUMP INTO THE EXISTING STORM

As a result, about four-in-ten asylum seekers in E___
(42%) were young men ages 18 to 34. This was al___

increase in asylum applicants of any EU
country. The number of asylum seekers
increased more than 800%, from more than
3,000 i   15. Meanwhile,
Hu   er of
as   m
4

& NOW
WATCH THE
SOUL'S
RELENTLESS
TRICKS &
DISGUISES

leading origin countries: 39% of those from Syria v
men, as were 38% of those from Afghanistan and ∠
from Iraq. Young adult males made up a larger sha
seek   tries. For example,
                                  (80%), Pa
                                  en in 2∘

THAT ENABLE
iT TO KEEP
iTs SECRETS

244

CARDBOARD

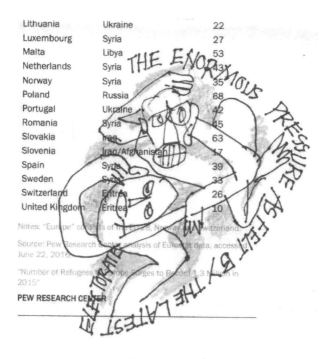

Lithuania	Ukraine	22
Luxembourg	Syria	27
Malta	Libya	53
Netherlands	Syria	43
Norway	Syria	35
Poland	Russia	68
Portugal	Ukraine	42
Romania	Syria	45
Slovakia	Iraq	63
Slovenia	Iraq/Afghanistan	17
Spain	Syria	39
Sweden	Syria	33
Switzerland	Eritrea	26
United Kingdom	Eritrea	10

Notes: "Europe" consists of the EU-28, Norway and Switzerland.

Source: Pew Research Center analysis of Eurostat data, accessed June 22, 2016

"Number of Refugees to Europe Surges to Record 1.3 Million in 2015"

PEW RESEARCH CENTER

arch.org

Iraq-Finland	20,000	2
Iraq-Sweden	20,000	2
Kosovo-Germany	33,000	3
Kosovo-Hungary	24,000	2
Albania-Germany	54,000	4
Nigeria-Italy	18,000	1

Note: "Europe" consists of the EU-28, Norway and Switzerland.
Rounded to nearest thousand. Percentages calculated from
unrounded numbers. Only top country pairs with the fewest asylum
seekers in 2015 shown. Sorted by the largest shares of all
Europe's asylum seekers in 2015.

Source: Pew Research Center analysis of Eurostat data accessed
June 22, 2016.

"Number of Refugees to Europe Surges to Record 1.3 Million in
2015"

PEW RESEARCH CENTER

people or 4% of all asylum applications.

ere the leading source countries after Syria in

within Europe.

WHO NEVERTHELESS
SUBMIT TO THE INDISCRIMINATE
GROWTH FACTOR OF THEIR
BELOVED ECONOMY

esearch.org

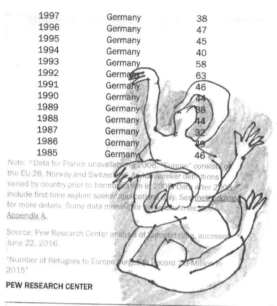

1997	Germany	38
1996	Germany	47
1995	Germany	45
1994	Germany	40
1993	Germany	58
1992	Germany	63
1991	Germany	46
1990	Germany	44
1989	Germany	38
1988	Germany	44
1987	Germany	32
1986	Germany	48
1985	Germany	46

Note: *Data for France unavailable in 2008. "Europe" consists of the EU-28, Norway and Switzerland. Asylum seeker definitions varied by country prior to harmonization in 2008. Data after 2008 include first-time asylum seeker applications only. See methodology for more details. Some data missing for some countries; see Appendix A.

Source: Pew Research Center analysis of Eurostat data, accessed June 22, 2016

"Number of Refugees to Europe Surges to Record 1.3 Million in 2015"

PEW RESEARCH CENTER

0s and 1990s may be lower if more data were available for all
ients of asylum seekers (Belgium, France, Germany, the

REQUIRE A RADICAL
NEW RESPONSE :

earch.org

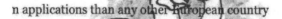

n applications than any other European country

Germany has been lead destination for asylum seekers most years since 1985

Country with largest number of asylum applications in Europe, by year

	Destination	%
2015	Germany	33
2014	Germany	29
2013	Germany	27
2012	Germany	
2011	France	18
2010	France	21
2009	France	18
2008*	UK	17
2007	Sweden	16
2006	France	15
2005	France	20
2004	France	20
2003	UK	16
2002	UK	22
2001	Germany	19
2000	UK	18
1999	Germany	22
1998	Germany	27

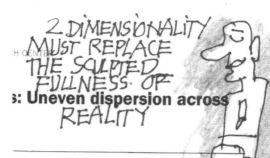

2 DIMENSIONALITY
MUST REPLACE
THE SCULPTED
FULLNESS OF

s: Uneven dispersion across

REALITY

Syria to Germany was the leading asylum seeker corridor in 2015

*Asylum seeker corridors of all first-time asylum
applicants in Europe, 2015*

Corridor	Total	% of all asylum applicants
Syria-Germany	159,000	12
Syria-Hungary	64,000	5
Syria-Sweden	51,000	4
Syria-Austria	25,000	2
Syria-Netherlands	19,000	1
Afghanistan-Hungary	46,000	3
Afghanistan-Sweden	41,000	3
Afghanistan-Germany	31,000	2
Afghanistan-Austria	25,000	2
Iraq-Germany	30,000	2

Syria was leading origin country for 13 out of 30 European countries in 2015

Top country of citizenship for first-time asylum applicants in each European country in 2015

Country of application	Top country of citizenship	% of all applications
Austria	Afghanistan	29
Belgium	Syria	26
Bulgaria	Iraq	34
Croatia	Syria	12
Cyprus	Syria	
Czech Republic	Ukraine	46
Denmark	Syria	41
Estonia	Ukraine	42
Finland	Iraq	63
France	Sudan	8
Germany	Syria	36
Greece	Syria	29
Hungary	Syria	37
Ireland	Pakistan	41
Italy	Nigeria	21
Latvia	Iraq	26

& WILL PROVIDE CITIZENS A FINE NEW IDENTITY OPPOSITE THEIR FORMER ANIMAL MUSCLED SUPERFICIALITY

The intensity of 2015's sudden migration of asylum seekers was felt more acutely in some European countries than in others. By far, Hungary (1,770 per 100,000 in Hungary's population), Sweden (1,600 per 100,000) and Austria (1,000 per 100,000) felt the effects of the asylum seeker surge the most in 2015. Germany (540 per 100,000) had a higher per capita number of asylum applicants than Europe (250 per 100,000) as a whole and was similar to other leading destinations such as Finland (590 per 100,000), Norway (590 per 100,000) and Switzerland (460 per 100,000). By contrast, France (110 per 100,000) and the UK (60 per 100,000) had a far lower per capita number of asylum seekers.

Syrian refugees did not evenly disperse in Europe

3. Europe's asylum seeker flow
Europe

Asylum seekers make their way to Europe in fits
and starts, by direct as well as indirect routes,
by air, land and sea. Consequently, it is difficult
to trace the precise paths taken by thousands of
asylum seekers. However, by pairing the
country where a migrant is seeking asylum with
the country that same migrant lists as country
of citizenship, it is possible to identify "bilateral
migration corridors" – i.e., flows between
points of origin and destination. These
corridors can provide a sense for who is seeking
asylum where.

In the case of Syrian refugees moving between
the Middle East and Europe in 2015, fully 84%
applied for asylum in just five countries

Prior to 2000, Germany annually had more asylu — a pattern extending back, uninterrupted, to 1985. These asylum seekers were from a range of countries, and many came from other European countries after the collapse of the Eastern Bloc in the early 1990s and the destabilization of the former Yugoslavia. In that decade for several years in the 1990s and 1990, Germany's overall share of asylum applications was roughly half or more of all of Europe's asylum applications.

FREE FROM THE ILL EFFECTS OF OVERWEIGHT & OVERABUNDANCE

A temporary shift in the leading countries of application occurred in the early 2000s. In 2000, 2002 and 2003, the UK became the leading destination country of asylum seekers in Europe, many of whom came from Iraq and Somalia. Between 2004 and 2011, France was often the leading destination. Many of these asylum seekers came from the Democratic Republic of the Congo, Haiti, Russia, Turkey and countries of the former Yugoslavia.

Germany resumed its previous part as the leading recipient of asylum applications in 2012, largely due to the growing number of asylum seekers from other European countries such as Kosovo, Russia and Serbia as well as countries such as Afghanistan, Iran, Iraq, Pakistan and Syria.

It is notable that the share of asylum seekers more recently applying in Germany is more on par with the share of asylum applications for Germany prior to 2000.[3] Since 2013, Germany

---

[3] The share of asylum seekers applying for asylum in Germany in the 1 European countries. Nonetheless, data for countries with the largest re Netherlands, Spain, Sweden and the UK) were available for most years

www.pewr

256

(Germany, Hungary, Sweden, Austria and the Netherlands). The Syria-Germany corridor was the most active one in 2015, with 159,000 Syrians seeking asylum in Germany. Other major corridors included Syria-Hungary (64,000 asylum seekers), Iraq-Germany (54,000) and Syria-Sweden (51,000).

Syria has been the point of origin for the largest asylum seeker corridors during the past few years. That was the case in 2014, when Europe's largest asylum seeker corridor was Syria to Germany, with 39,000 applicants or 7% of asylum applications in Europe. In 2013, the Syria-Sweden corridor was the largest asylum seeker flow, numbering 17,000

Afghanistan, Iraq, Kosovo, Albania and Nigeria w 2015 for asylum seeker flows to specific countries

As suggested above, Syrian and other asylum
seekers have tended to concentrate along
specific migration corridors en route to
Europe. This has contributed to the uneven
distribution of asylum seekers across the EU-
28, Norway and Switzerland. In some
countries, particular groups make up a sizable
portion of all asylum seekers, even when the
countries in question are not part of Europe's
main refugee corridors.

In 2015, Syria was the leading source country
of asylum seekers in 13 out of 30 European
countries. Among those few citizen
countries Syrians also constituted a third or
more of asylum seekers in Romania (45%),
Cyprus (41%), the Netherlands..., Denmark

& IN RESPONSE TO INVASIONS FROM ABOVE WHEN ONLY FLATNESS CAN SAVE YOU FROM THE HORROR OF REFUGEEDOM

www.pewr

258

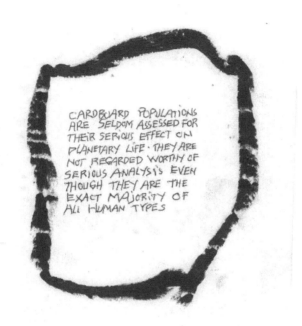

CARDBOARD POPULATIONS
ARE SELDOM ASSESSED FOR
THEIR SERIOUS EFFECT ON
PLANETARY LIFE. THEY ARE
NOT REGARDED WORTHY OF
SERIOUS ANALYSIS EVEN
THOUGH THEY ARE THE
EXACT MAJORITY OF
ALL HUMAN TYPES

CARDBOARD'S STRENGTH IS
THAT IT ISN'T IN THE
THINKING OF REALITY
PHILOSOPHERS. ITS ABILITY
TO BE NEGLECTED

THE POPULATION SAYS:
WE WHO SUFFER NORMALITY-
REALITY KNOW CARDBOARD
VERY WELL & ARE CONVINCED
OF ITS EXISTENTIAL POWER

WE WHO CONFESS TO BE
CARDBOARD OR SIMILAR TO it
BY BIRTH & ASSIGNMENT
NEED TO ADDRESS YOUR
HIGHNESSES THE FLESH
& BLOOD IDIOTS OF CURRENT
REALITY

THE CARDBOARD PHENOMENON

WE WANT TO BUT
CANNOT BE HAPPY
IN THE CARDBOARD
REPUBLIC
THE 2-DIMENSIONALITY
OF THE CIRCUMSTANCES
DOES NOT RELIEVE
OUR PAIN BUT
MAKES it WORSE

WE SISTERS &
BROTHERS in CARDBOARD
HAVE OUR SOULS PERMA
NENTLY PUT ON EDGE &
RIDICULED BY CARDBOARD
& ITS CRUEL NONCHALANCE

WE ARE ASSIGNED
CARDBOARD STATUS IN
COMPLIANCE WITH THE
CARDBOARD REPUBLIC...
& WITH THAT ARE THE
TYPICAL COLLABORATORS
OF WAR & CRIME

FINALLY
THE POPULA-
TION GETS
CORNERED

& BECOMES THAT
PART OF ITSELF THAT
CONFORMS WITH
POLICE
LAW
& BRUTALITY

THE MIRACLE GODS
& SUPERIORS OF THE
DEMOCRACY SYSTEM
KEEP TRYING TO BE
THE PERMANENT
DOMINEERERS OF
THE LITTLE HUMANS
WITH THEIR CHANGING
ADMINISTRATIONS

BUT

THE HORRENDOUS
EFFECTS OF THE
ADMINISTRATION'S
FAILURES & MISHAPS
DISALLOW THE
POPULATION'S
SATISFACTION &
DWINDLE THE GODS
& THEIR MIRACLES
TILL THEY ARE
MERE SPECKS
OF DUST

BUT EVEN UNDER THESE
CIRCUMSTANCES THE UNSIGHTLY
PART OF REALITY PUSHES ITS
IMAGERY UNTO PUBLIC PERCEPTION
& DOESN'T ALLOW THE THEORISTS
TO GET AWAY WITH THEIR
PROPAGANDA

TYPICAL REALITY CITIZENS
CROWD THE RUSH HOUR TRAFFIC
WITHOUT NOTICING OLD MR. & MRS.
REALITY LIMPING PAINFULLY
SLOWLY AMIDST THE HIGHSPEED
WORKFORCE MEMBERS
DISSEMINATING THEIR ESSENCE
WITHOUT PROPAGANDA

RESTING PRECARIOUSLY ON A
CARDBOARD BOX LISTENING TO THE
AWAKENING CARDBOARD SPIRITS
WHO ARE READY TO JUMP TO THEIR
FEET GRIMACING & GROWLING

AS THEY CONFRONT

THE ONEDIRECTIONAL
WORKFORCE MARCH

WITH
THEIR

JOLLY

OPPOSITION

In April and May this year, 1 in 17 migrants
African coast to Italy. That was more than t
Geneva-based International Organization f

Nearly 2,700 people are known to have diec
crossing, well above the 1,970 fatalities on a
months of 2015.

The "increasingly deadly" route across the c
"major humanitarian crisis," the IOM warn

Migrants seeking a new life in the Europear
callous people-smugglers, says Jens Pagotto
search-and-rescue ship operated by Doctor:
based humanitarian aid organization, off th

But these dramas are only now attracting re
recently, the tragedies in the central Medite

THE CARDBOARD CITIZENS
OF THE CARDBOARD REPUBLIC
DO THEIR CHORES

The rising death rate, however, is a result ⊂
boats and the catastrophic overloading of i
but crammed with as many as 150, accordi

immediate 'conditions of distress'
No longer do people-smugglers carry refug
home to Libya for another consignment.

Instead they pack boats with passengers, l
international waters, give basic instruction
direction to head in, and then cast the mig

"It is not the intention that these boats ma
"They are designed to reach ... the high sea
operation."

Sometimes the smugglers leave a satellite t
number for the Italian maritime rescue cer

& WAGE-LABOR DUTIFULLY
CAREFULLY

Mediterranean has risen to record highs. "
argues Pagotto. "You cannot solve this pro

Doctors Without Borders announced recer
in protest against the deal with Turkey to s
consideration of their asylum claims. The o
establish safe, legal routes for refugees tha
lethal risks.

Pagotto acknowledges, however, that "the p
easy solution" that would prevent tens of tl
Europe every year.

The EU report found that "the majority of r
sub-Saharan West Africans, who generally
under EU asylum rules. It pointed out that
brought to Italy apply for asylum upon arri
rejected, indicating that the majority of arr
rather than refugees fleeing war or politica

LIKE ANY CITIZEN
WITH ONE ADDED APPREHENSION:
RAIN

across the Mediterranean Sea has sur[
spokesman for the United Nations' ref
3,800 have died attempting the voyag[

And that number could rise further. M
dead after their boat sank in the Medit
coast guard spokesman, Ayoub Qasser
said at least 29 migrants have been re[
had been on the inflatable boat, appar[
Italy.

All told, only about a third as many mi
year compared with last year. That me
about migration dynamics has change[
times as deadly.

The reasons are manifold. They stem f
hard-nosed decisions by governments,
consequences of reckless decisions by
serve as a basis for understanding the

BUT THEY ARE WHAT
THEY ARE & THEY HAVE

SURVIVED

number of arrivals in Greece," suggests Joe

At the same time, he points out, migrant bo
sporadically off the Libyan coast for the pas
outrage."

That is especially true when victims' bodies
accessible Turkish beaches – as was the cas
September – but wash up instead on inacce

Since Turkey agreed last March to take bacl
and the EU promised in return to give Anka
stuck on Turkish soil, refugee flows into Gr
by 90 percent.

But the number of European arrivals from I
route starts, has held steady in recent years
almost all of them from sub-Saharan Africa
same number as came during the same peri

JUST AS WE SURVIVE OUR DISASTERS & WARS

to tell somebody that they exist.

"The traffickers put people out to sea very ⌷
moment they leave," says the IOM's Mr. M⌷
Libya is counting the seconds till the rescu⌷

An international flotilla of vessels is patroll⌷
search of migrants in distress – Italian coa⌷
naval force, and private ships operated by ⌷
Doctors Without Borders.

They do not find everybody in need, and sc⌷
weekend, between Friday and Monday, sea⌷
On June 23 alone, the Italian coast guard r⌷
rescued from 43 different boats.

"None of those craft could have made the c⌷

Rising death toll

WITHOUT EVER LEARNING
ANYTHING BETTER THAN
SURVIVABILITY

That is of no consequence to Pagotto, who
desperate migrants he plucks from the sea.

"At the end of the day," he says, "they are a

https://www.washingtonpost.com/news/w
mediterranean-sea-crossings-were-three-ti

WorldViews

A shipwreck off Libya rai

death toll for migrants in

By Max Bearak and Brian Murphy October 2

There are more than two months left i
have died this year trying to reach Eur

assed last year's grim total. A
ugee agency said Wednesday that
e this year.

ore than 90 migrants are feared
erranean east of Tripoli, a Libyan
n, said Thursday. The coast guard
cued, but survivors said 126 people
ently seeking to reach either Malta or

grants have tried the sea crossing this
ans something
d to make reaching Europe three

rom the unintended consequences of
, as well as the inevitable
smugglers. Below is a map that can
shift in migration that has taken place

& THAT'S EXACTLY HOW
CARDBOARD WORKS:

the use of increasingly unseaworthy
latables designed to hold 30 passengers
; to people involved in rescue efforts.

s to the Italian coast and then return

l just enough fuel for them to reach
on how the engine works and which
its loose.

it to Europe," a recent EU report found.
to then trigger a search and rescue

ephone with their clients, along with a
r in Rome, so that the refugees can call

BARE MINIMUM SURVIVABI
LITY IN PRECARIOUS &
DANGEROUS CIRCUMSTANCES

search and rescue is not the solution,"
blem at sea."

tly it would no longer accept EU funding,
end back refugees without any serious
rganization is calling on the EU to
would deter them from taking potentially

problem is so complex there is no single
iousands of Africans from trying to reach

nigrants rescued at sea on this route are
speaking are not eligible for relocation"
"less than half of those rescued and
val, and a large majority of these are
ivals seem to be economic migrants,"
persecution.

OFTEN REFERRED TO
AS JUNK OR GARBAGE

died trying to make it from the North
wice the 2015 death rate, according to the
or Migration (IOM)

l so far this year trying to make the
ll Mediterranean routes in the first seven

entral Mediterranean has become a
d in a recent report.

Union "are being sent to their deaths" by
, head of mission for the "Aquarius," a
Without Borders (MSF), the Geneva-
Libyan coast.

ewed public attention in Europe. Until
ranean were "overwhelmed by the

BUT ACTUALLY GIFTED
WITH ALL THE EXQUISITE
SENSIBILITIES OF THE
2 DIMENSIONAL ARTS

ENDLESSLY PROLIFIC &
ENDLESSLY EXPRESSIVE OF
INSUBORDINATE LIFE

oe-migrant-crisis-sees-spike-in-deadly-Mediterranean-

is sees spike in
in crossings

as dropped 90 percent, but North Africans are
worthy boats.

rch has stemmed the flood of refugees
, but overall the continent's migrant crisis

till attempting to cross the Mediterranean
dying.

FLYING LESSON N°5

FLYING LESSON No 6

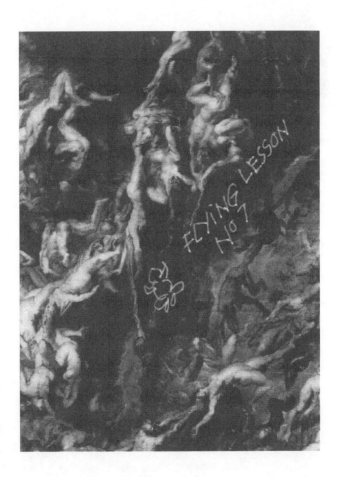

POPULATION
THOUGHTS

POPULATION THOUGHTS & PREOCCUPATIONS

299

300

COPS

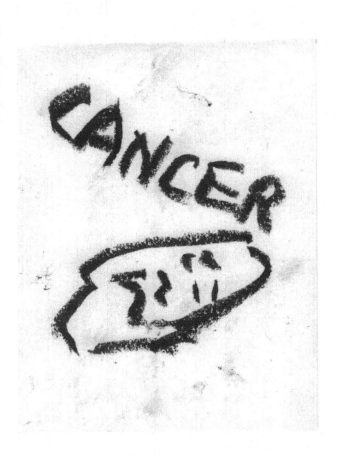

POPULATION CONFUSIONS

1. HORIZONTALISM & VERTICALISM

2. GOD CATASTROPHE & THE MEANING OF THE ABOVE

3. EXCELLENCE ECSTASY & PERFECTIONISM

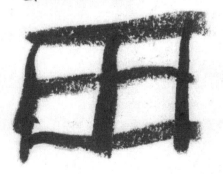

WE ARE IN THE POPULA
TION YOU ARE IN THE POP
ULATION WE ARE THE
POPULATION OUR EGOS
HAVE BEEN IDENTIFIED .
AS BUILDING BLOCS FOR
POPULATION
OUR INDIVIDUALISM is
DECIDED BY POPULATION
NEEDS & WISHES
OUR SHOPPINGS ARE THE
EXPRESSION OF PARTICIPATION
IN POPULATION .

GODS

THE AUTHORITIES IN CAHOOTS WITH THE GODS WHO HELPED THEM TO GET THE AUTHORITY JOB, PERMANENTLY NEED DIVINE BACKUP FOR THEIR SCHEMES IN ORDER TO NOT BE PERCEIVED AS NOTHING BUT MONEY ARE UTTERLY CONFUSED WHEN THESE GODS UNLEASH THEIR FURY IN EXACTLY THE WRONG PLACE & USE THEIR CATASTROPHES AGAINST THE LEAST DESERVING AS IF WANTING TO ELIMINATE ANY TRACE OF A RECOGNIZABLE DIVINE JUSTICE SYSTEM & THEN THE QUESTION IS: SHOULD THESE GODS WHO DISPLAY SUCH SENSELESS BEHAVIOR BE KEPT IN POWER? ARE THEY INCOMPETENT OR DISINTERESTED?

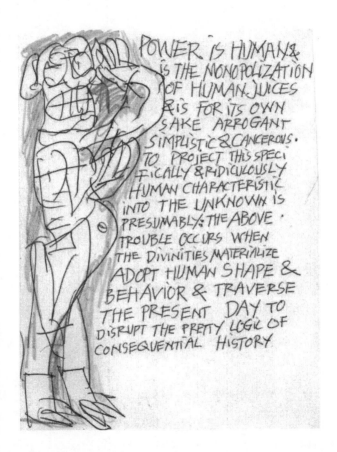

POWER IS HUMAN &
IS THE MONOPOLIZATION
OF HUMAN JUICES
& IS FOR ITS OWN
SAKE ARROGANT
SIMPLISTIC & CANCEROUS.
TO PROJECT THIS SPECI
FICALLY & RIDICULOUSLY
HUMAN CHARACTERISTIC
INTO THE UNKNOWN IS
PRESUMABLY; THE ABOVE ·
TROUBLE OCCURS WHEN
THE DIVINITIES MATERIALIZE
ADOPT HUMAN SHAPE &
BEHAVIOR & TRAVERSE
THE PRESENT DAY TO
DISRUPT THE PRETTY LOGIC OF
CONSEQUENTIAL HISTORY

OUR LIFE IS NOT
THE LEAST BIT
WHAT WE COULD
REASONABLY
EXPECT IT TO BE.
IT SOARED IN
STORMY SKIES WAS
DOWNED BY WAR&HUNGER
STARTED AGAIN & AGAIN
FROM ALMOST NOWHERE
SUCCEEDING & FAILING ROUTINELY
BUT NEVER SUCCEEDING TO
COLLECT THE GOODS OF THE
STRIFE NEVER INSPIRED
ENOUGH TO DEFEAT THE
INHERITED DOWNTRODDENESS
THAT IS THE HUMAN TRADEMARK
THAT'S WHERE THE GODS
COME IN!

THE GODS WHO TRADI
TIONALLY KEEP A PRE
SENCE ON EARTH ONLY
NOT HUGE AS MIGHT BE
EXPECTED NOT AUTHORI
TATIVELY CORRECT BUT
RATHER MODEST NOT
IN ORDER TO BE TORTURED
& KILLED FOR THEOLOGICAL
PURPOSES & YET TORTURED
& KILLED FREQUENTLY

AS A BYPRODUCT OF
NONCONFORMING BEHA
VIOR MOSTLY ACT ON
BEHALF OF EXTINCT
GOING NONPOLITICISED
SPECIES THE HUMAN
ANIMALS (CATEGORIZED
SIMPLY AS ANIMALS).
FISHLIKE GODS HAVE
BEEN SEEN OBSTRUCTING
FISHFACTORY EXPLOITS.
FLYING GODS HAVE
MINGLED WITH OFFCOURSE
MIGRATING FLOCKS.

CRAWLING GODS HAVE JOINED HABITAT DEPRIVED REPTILES & DIVINE VISITS ARE MOTIVATED BY RECENT WARS & DEVASTATIONS THAT ARE USUALLY BLAMED ON RADICAL ELEMENTS BUT ARE SERIOUSLY LOGICAL CONSEQUENCES OF THE MODERNIZATION OF HUMAN LIFE, GENERALLY REFERRED TO AS PROGRESS

YES

THESE POORLY DRESSED
OFTEN LIMPING GODS
WHO ARE INDISTINGUI-
SHABLE FROM THE HEART
RENDING SUFFERERS
WHO ROAM THE EARTH
LIKE AN ANCIENT BREED
OF NOT BELONGING HALF
BROKEN SOULS WHO FIT
NOWHERE IN THE CONSTI-
TUTIONS OF NATIONS ARE
NEITHER ALLOWED TO
STOP NOR TO GO ON.

THESE GODS WHO SHARE
THE FATE OF THE CAPSIZED
THRONGS ON THE TERRIBLE
SEA & SWIM & DROWN
WITH THE SWIMMING &
DROWNING CHILDREN &
THEIR MOTHERS ARE
THE SAME WHO WILL
LATER MAKE TROUBLE
IN THE REFUGEE CAMPS
ORGANIZE PROTEST HUNGER
STRIKES & REVOLTS & DON'T
ALLOW WATCHFUL EYES &
CONSCIENCES TO GET AWAY
FROM THE ISSUE

OTHERS VERY SLOW &
OBVIOUSLY UNDERNOURISHED
GODS   HAVE BEEN
SEEN   SLIPPING BY
THE   GUARDS
OF   PARLIA
MENTAR   Y PALACES
MAKIN   G THEIR
WAY   INTO THE
CONFER   ENCES OF
THE CON   CERNED
BRANCHES OF GOVERNMENT
NEVER RAISING THEIR VOICE
NEVER SPEAKING A WORD BUT BY
THEIR PRESENCE EFFECTING THE HEARTS
OF REFUGEE SPECIALISTS
TO WHAT AVAIL IS NOT YET KNOWN

PORTRAITS OF HARDTRYING SEMI EFFECTIVE GODS

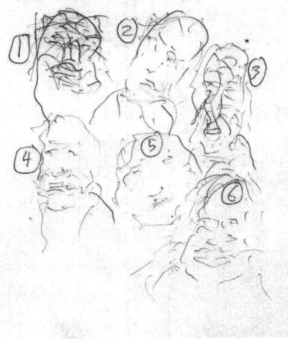

BUT THE ODDEST
CONTINGENT OF THESE
ITINERANT GODS ARE
THOSE WHO ACT AS
ADVERTISING AGENTS

THE ONES WHO
MINGLE LEISURELY
& EASILY SO AS TO
MAKE THEIR POINT
WHICH IS DEEPLY RE
LATED TO REFUGEEDOM

DRAWING ATTENTION TO
THE PAINED TOOLS OF
REFUGEEDOM : THE OVER
WORKED HANDS & FEET OF
DISCARDED NEGLECTED DIS-
USED UNRECOGNIZED
IMPORTANCE & IN NEED OF
THE AGENTS' PRO-FOOT
PRO-HAND ADVERTISEMENT
WHICH POSITIVELY AUGMENTS
THE SHEER MUSCLE POWER
& MUSCLE JOY OF THESE
APPENDIXES & URGES USE
OVERUSE & TRAINING TO
REALIZE THEIR SENSUOUS
PRODUCTIVITY, REALIZE THEIR
EGO, GO TO THEM INDULGE
IN THEM EDUCATE & DISTILL

THEIR POTENTIAL, CHANT &
DANCE FOR THEM 'ADVERTISE
THEIR GREATNESS THEIR
INSTINCTIVE OPPOSITION TO
MACHINERY THEIR SPORTSMAN
SHIP WHICH INCLUDES ALL THE
REFLECTIVE PAUSES NEEDED
FOR RECUPERATION

THIS
MEANS

THESE ADVERTISEMENT
AGENT GODS WALK AMONGST
THE DEPRIVED & WARTORN
NOTHINGS WHO WERE FORCED
TO BE REFUGEES & IN THE
MIDST OF THE HORRENDOUS
DISTRESS ADVERTISE THE
QUALITY OF DISTRESS
THE ADVANTAGE OF PHYSICAL
ENGAGEMENT OVER THE
ABSENCE OF THE PHYSICAL

NATURALLY YOU CAN'T GET
ANY WHERE WITH THIS KIND
OF TALK · THE CUSTOMERS
DISMISS YOU & HATE YOU
BECAUSE THEY KNOW YOU
ARE SPEAKING TRUTH TO
BITTER CIRCUMSTANCE.
REFUGEES HAVE NO TIME
FOR ELEMENTARY REFLECTIONS

THEY NEED
TO LIVE

LIFE MEANS WHATEVER it
MEANS AT THE TIME
CIVILIZATION COUCH COFFEE
THE TOTAL THE UNNECESSARY
AS WELL AS THE NECESSARY
THEY ESCAPEES FROM MOTHER
DEATH KNOW & YOU GOD OR
NO GOD SHUT UP ONLY I THE
SUFFERER KNOWS
THE INCOMPETENT GODS COME
& GO AWARE OF THEIR NEAR
ZERO SUCCESS RATE
NOBODY KNOWS WHAT
WOULD HAPPEN IF THEY
WOULDN'T COME

333

334

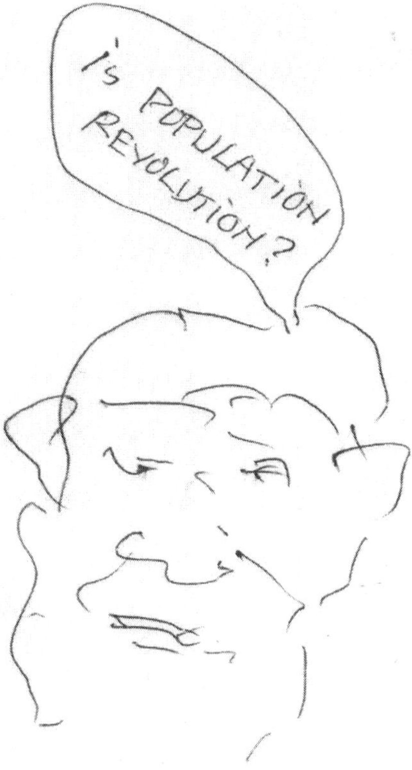
IS POPULATION REVOLUTION?

WHAT PREVENTS REVOLUTION?

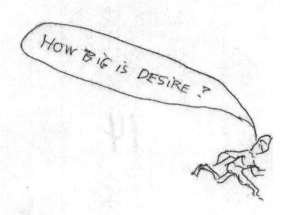

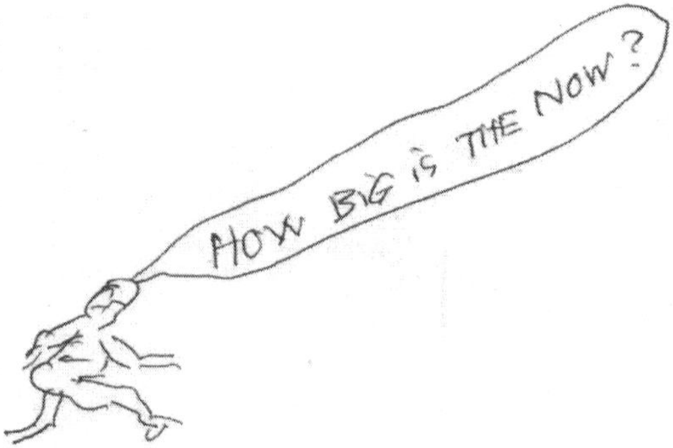
HOW BIG IS THE NOW?

343

346

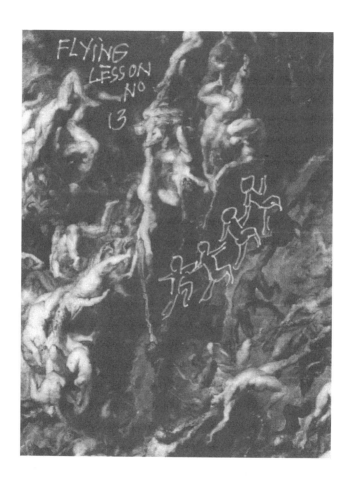

COULDN'T WE ALSO
TELL THEM SUFFICIENTLY
SKILLFULLY ABOUT THE
ANGELS & THE CLOUDS
BURSTING WITH INVISIBLE
LIFE FULL OF MEANING

COULDN'T WE ALSO
PROVIDE THE ENTICING
SMELL WHICH THE MESS
LIKES TO DIP ITSELF INTO

COULDN'T WE TOO GIVE THEM THE SUPER- NATURAL WORDS in front OF WHICH THEY KNEEL WITH ARTHRITIC KNEES

COULDN'T WE TOO
SWING & WAVE THE
HOLY FLAG THAT
CURDLES THE BLOOD
& CHEERS THE NEAR
iMPOSSiBLE

& THEN CONSEQUEN
TLY COULDN'T OUR
LIFE BE A LITTLE LESS
DEPRESSED THAN THAT
PARTICULAR MODEL
OF LIFE

THE WAVE

WE

WHEN
WE
ARE
A
WAVE

fear is hope.

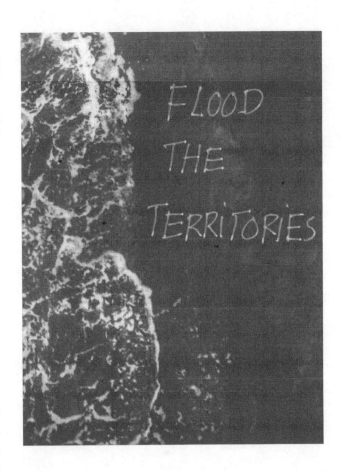

THE TERRITORIES
AWAKEN

THE AWAKENED TERRITORIES

THE

TERRITORIES

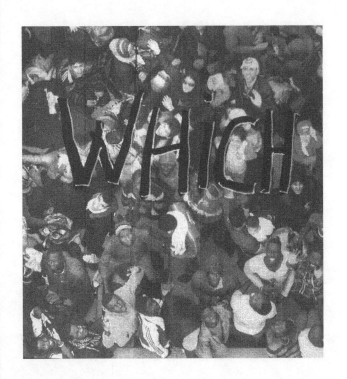

THEY

Mediterranean migration drives rise in deaths

Worldwide migration deaths are on the rise, driven by growing numbers of refugees lost at sea in the Mediterranean, according to new data from the International Organization for Migration (IOM). Tom Rollins reports.

More than 3,700 people died worldwide during migration in the first half of 2016, a 23-percent increase compared with the same period last year and a staggering 52-percent increase compared with 2014, according to the latest IOM data.

they need to rescue several thousand people on several hundred boats." That "mass embarkation" strategy has resulted in single-incident death tolls reaching into the hundreds.

More than 1,000 died off the Libyan coast in a single week in May. In September, 162 bodies were recovered from a wreck off the Egyptian coast. The incident that pushed this year's total over last year's occurred overnight Tuesday when a Doctors Without Borders rescue ship came across an inflatable dinghy with 107 live passengers and 25 dead ones. The dead were found crushed underfoot on the dinghy, in a pool of seawater mixed with fuel.

On Monday, about 2,200 migrants were rescued in the central Mediterranean in 21 operations. Only 16 bodies were recovered, according to the Italian coast guard, but a spokesman for the International Organization for Migration said survivors were certain that the toll was higher.

Crisis

Over 1,500 migrants have died trying to reach Europe—and the numbers are only likely to increase unless the EU takes real action

On April 19, more than 600 refugees drowned in the Mediterranean when their boat capsized on its way from Africa to Italy. On April 12, about 400 people died in a separate shipwreck. So far in 2015, 1,600 migrants have lost their lives trying to cross the Mediterranean, and authorities fear that the number will surge as the weather warms. These five stats explain the rising tide of migration problems for Europe and for the desperate migrants of Africa and the Middle East.

smuggler ran a trip from Egypt that ultimately sank off Malta in September 2014. Up to 500 people died at sea. One of the men Yousef was detained with back in Alexandria lost his wife and daughter in the tragedy.

Markus Schildhauer represents the German Seafarers' Association in Alexandria. He often meets with merchant crews returning to port and hears the stories of the sea.

"In the port, I meet so many traumatized seafarers," he told DW, referring to a growing trend of merchant vessels rescuing migrant boats at sea. "Either they where called to a rescue where people died, or they've heard about this and are afraid of it."

Sea crossings from Libya are notorious, and statistically far more dangerous than Egypt, despite the shorter distance. According to Amnesty International Libya researcher Mouna Elkekhia, refugees and migrants are "kept hostage in these houses or farms next to the sea until the smugglers get enough people ready to be piled into the rubber dinghies."

"It wasn't a sand beach...but behind a factory for something and there were big stones [on the shore]. We went down into the water until it was up to our trousers, then up to our necks. We were totally in the water."

Zaytouni's group were ferried bit-by-bit in a *hassakeh*, a small dinghy, out to a larger boat waiting off-shore. They were then taken to another, bigger boat waiting about an hour out to sea.

Groups of refugees had been waiting on the boat for weeks at a time, Zaytouni says, part of a time-tested Egyptian smuggling tactic designed to fill up a boat to maximum capacity before leaving. The tactic, known to some as *takhzeen* (literally, "in storage"), can prolong the crossing for days - even weeks - and means passengers sometimes run out of food and water before even leaving Egyptian waters.

Tragedy at sea

Zaitouni was later caught at sea by the Egyptian coastguard, after drifting in the Mediterranean for days punctuated only by burnt-out engines and boats swaying uncertainly out at sea.

One out of every 47 people attempting the crossing from North Africa has died, Spindler said. When the route to Greece was in full swing last year, that number was one in 269.

Almost 3,000 of those fatalities - 78 percent - occurred in the Mediterranean; many of them in waters connecting Egypt and Libya with Italy, otherwise known as the Central Mediterranean route.

IOM's analysis points to "several new and dangerous smuggling practices," including a practice of "sending migrants in unseaworthy vessels," or smugglers sending out multiple boats at once, "making search-and-rescue operations more complicated."

"New routes are also increasingly risky: particularly when boats depart from Egypt, the journey is longer, and search and rescue is often carried out further away from land," IOM added.

In one case reported by Amnesty, the coastguard deserted a boat full of people that they'd initially stopped at sea, leaving 120 people stranded onboard

"One of the men from the Libyan coastguard boat came onto our boat to drive it back to Libya. He drove it nearly half way back, but then the motor stopped working," Mohamed, a 26-year-old Eritrean man told Amnesty. "I heard him say, 'If you die, you die,' before getting back on his boat and driving away, leaving us stuck in the sea.

Many Syrians found refuge in surrounding countries like Turkey — which hosts 1.6 million Syrian refugees— and Egypt, Lebanon and Jordan. But conditions for many refugees in those countries have become more difficult in recent months. Egypt has altered its migrant policy, including by imposing visa obligations and revoking residence permits. Similar policies have been implemented recently in Lebanon and Jordan. New migrant policies in Iran have additionally led many Afghans who had found refuge in the neighboring country to seek their fortunes in Europe.

It is now estimated that for every 1,000 migrants that are known to have crossed the Mediterranean, more than 46 lose their lives in shipwrecks. The actual number might even be higher.

Many say that number may continue to rise. Officials in Greece project the arrival of up to 100,000 migrants in 2015. Current trends confirm these calculations: during the first quarter of 2015, more than 10,000 migrants arrived in the country, the head of the Greek office of the IOM told HuffPost. These high numbers are unusual, since the primary season for migrant activity is usually from June to November.

Not much better on land

And while smugglers and traffickers in Libya are notorious, so too are coastguards and prison guards operating near the shore. A recent Amnesty International report, featuring interviews with 90 survivors who made it to Italy, documented "abhorrent human rights violations" carried out by Libya's coastguard or inside immigration detention facilities that included shootings, beatings and all-out torture.

SAVED AT SEA

July 6: 3.5 hours, 3 rescues, 366 saved
Rescue No. 1
- Inflatable dinghy, detected 3:45 a.m.
- 5 women
- 102 men
- 1 baby

Rescue No. 2

- Inflatable dinghy, detected 7:10 a.m.
- 1 woman
- 124 men
- No children

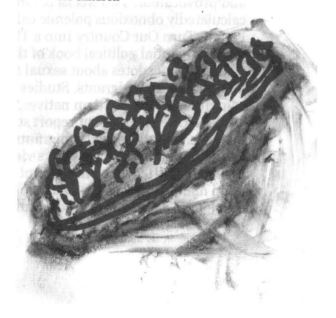

Rescue No. 3
- Inflatable dinghy, detected 7:10 a.m.
- 53 women
- 76 men
- 4 children

412

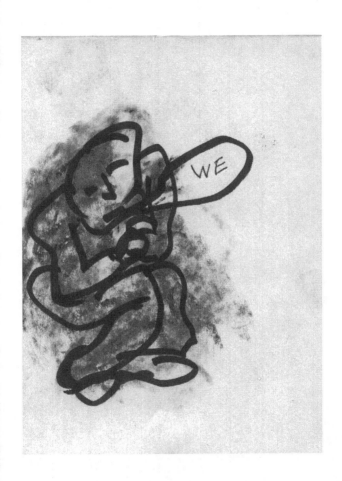

414

415

421

423

429

thanks to Marc &
Donna for edit &
design
to Esfeh for scanning
& to P. P. Rubens
for the fall of the
rebel angels

Pe Schn

A visitor to the Bread & Puppet Museum will find a vast array of masks, sculptures, paintings and puppets – from inches to yards tall --depicting what Donna and I collectively refer to as "population" – images of vulnerable humanity.

Across half a century of the theater's work these figures, and those who oppress them, have been the pervasive characters of Peter Schumann's concern, present in hundreds of forms, the background and face of his universe.

But recently, the background has arisen, and broken into the foreground -- as refugees created by US-spawned chaos, the truly "wretched of the earth", have desperately crossed borders seeking safety and a temporary home. The consequences, along with climate mayhem, will define our 21st century.

Peter Schuman, himself once a refugee, has compressed his analysis and his rage into this little book.

Marc Estrin and Donna Bister
Fomite Press